A. B. SIMPSON
AND THE PENTECOSTAL MOVEMENT

A. B. Simpson
and the
Pentecostal
Movement

A Study in Continuity, Crisis, and Change

Charles W. Nienkirchen

HENDRICKSON
PUBLISHERS
PEABODY, MASSACHUSETTS 01961-3473

Copyright © 1992 by Hendrickson Publishers, Inc.
P. O. Box 3473
Peabody, Massachusetts, 01961–3473
All rights reserved
Printed in the United States of America

ISBN 0–913573–99–X

Library of Congress Cataloging-in-Publication Data

Nienkirchen, Charles W.
    A. B. Simpson and the Pentecostal movement: a study in
continuity, crisis, and change / Charles W. Nienkirchen.
        p.   cm.
    Includes index.
    ISBN 0–913573–99–X (pbk.)
    1. Simpson, A. B. (Albert B.) 2. Pentecostalism—History.
3. Christian and Missionary Alliance—History. I. Title.
BX6700.Z8S562   1992
289.9—dc20
[B]   92-13672
                                                                CIP

To my dear wife, Gwen,
and to my children, Charity, Caleb, and Bethany,
who have persevered through everything
necessary for me to write a book

CONTENTS

ACKNOWLEDGMENTS

GOOD BOOKS ARE NOT singular efforts. I am indebted to many who have both made possible and immeasurably enhanced the quality of this work.

Rev. John Sawin, Alliance pastor, missionary, historian, archivist, and friend, passed on to me his passion for studying Alliance history and guided me in the acquisition and interpretation of early Alliance source materials.

Dr. and Mrs. Del Fredlund of Saskatoon, Saskatchewan, generously underwrote both the expenses of research trips to Nyack, New York, Springfield, Missouri, and Tulsa, Oklahoma, and other costs incurred during the preparation of the text.

Dr. Gary McGee, Professor of Church History at the Assemblies of God Theological Seminary in Springfield, Missouri, graciously read parts of the first draft of the manuscript and offered valuable insights into those Alliance/Pentecostal persons whose lives embraced both movements.

Dr. Walter Hollenweger, formerly of the University of Birmingham, England, gave encouragement and direction.

Those who facilitated the researching of the book include: Sandy Ayer, Director of Library Services, Canadian Bible College/Canadian Theological Seminary, Regina, Saskatchewan; Lynn Anderson, Director of the Myer Pearlman Memorial Library, Central Bible College, Springfield, Missouri; Wayne Warner, Director of the Assemblies of God Archives, Springfield, Missouri; Karen Jermyn, Director of the Holy Spirit Research Center, Oral Roberts University, Tulsa, Oklahoma; Ron McMillan, Registrar of the Keswick Convention, Keswick, England; and the numerous librarians of the Bodleian and British Museum libraries in Oxford and London, England.

Lynn Munson and Avril Dyson entered the first and final drafts of the text into their word processors.

Last but not least, my thanks to Patrick Alexander, my general editor at Hendrickson, who has overseen the finished version and tolerated my tardy deadlines.

PREFACE

IN MANY RESPECTS THE PROCESS that gave birth to this study mirrors the subject under consideration. Since the book deals with the historical relationship between two movements, the Christian and Missionary Alliance (primarily its founder) and twentieth-century Pentecostalism, fittingly it also has a dual Alliance and Pentecostal heritage. The first inspiration to research and write on this topic came as the fruit of many conversations with colleagues, students, Alliance clergy, laypersons, missionaries, and denominational leaders while serving on the faculties of Canadian Bible College and Canadian Theological Seminary in Regina, Saskatchewan. Coediting and contributing to a collection of articles on the life and ministry of Albert Benjamin Simpson, published by the faculty of Canadian Theological Seminary in anticipation of the Alliance's centennial celebrations in 1987, provided the context for my first substantive investigation of Simpson's responses to the Pentecostal movement.

Pentecostals also share in the inspiration for this volume. During the dialogue that followed my presentation of a paper entitled "A. B. Simpson: Forerunner of the Modern Pentecostal Movement," at the Society for Pentecostal Studies meeting held in Costa Mesa, California, in 1986, I observed that Pentecostal historians, like many Alliance persons, were unaware of the full scope of Simpson's attitude to Pentecostalism. Consequently the desire to write a book that would serve both Alliance and Pentecostal constituencies was further heightened.

As I located and delved into the primary sources, I became particularly intrigued by those persons whose spiritual aspirations motivated them to make the trek from Old Orchard Beach to Azusa Street, metaphorically speaking. In going on this journey they came to regard the Alliance and Pentecostal traditions not as mutually exclusive denominational entities but rather as successive phases of a deeper Christian life they were experiencing at a time of steadily intensifying worldwide spiritual awakening.

The passage of time allows denominations to erect doctrinal walls between themselves and those from whom they wish to be distinguished, a process in which political expediency plays no small part. The history of renewal movements, especially in their first generation, however, shows that a concern with having vital religious experience takes precedence over establishing a rigid doctrinal identity. The leaders of these movements are invariably spiritual pilgrims first and systematic theologians second. The lives of Albert Benjamin Simpson and Pentecostal pioneers bear eloquent testimony to this.

In order to make Simpson more directly accessible to the reader, I have included as appendixes some of the Alliance Founder's lesser known (and harder to obtain) but most important writings regarding the Pentecostal movement. These sources, consisting of a hitherto unpublished diary, excerpts from annual presidential reports, and a selection of editorials, allow the reader to hear Simpson speak for himself.

While death ends a life, it does not necessarily end a relationship. The founder and his denomination are still in dialogue. The vitality of Simpson's spiritual journey lives on and continues to speak to a current generation of Alliance adherents. In my own case, the actual retracing of Simpson's footsteps in New York City during Advent season, 1988, encouraged me to make life-changing decisions that have led deeper into a life of expectant faith.

Charles Nienkirchen, Ph.D.
King's Fold Center of Retreat and Renewal
Cochrane, Alberta, Canada

ABBREVIATIONS

AR   *Annual Report of the Christian and Missionary Alliance*
AW   *Alliance Weekly*
CA   *Christian Alliance*
CAFMW   *Christian Alliance and Foreign Missionary Weekly*
CAMW   *Christian Alliance and Missionary Weekly*
CE   *Christian Evangel*
CMAW   *Christian and Missionary Alliance Weekly*
DPCM   *Dictionary of Pentecostal and Charismatic Movements*, ed.
        Stanley M. Burgess and Gary B. McGee (Grand
        Rapids: Zondervan, 1988)
LT   *Living Truths*
ND   A. B. Simpson's Nyack Diary (1907–16), unpublished
        typed copy available in the archives of Canadian
        Bible College/Canadian Theological Seminary,
        Regina, Saskatchewan, Canada.
PE   *Pentecostal Evangel*
SS   "Simpson Scrapbook," comp. C. Donald McKaig,
        unpublished typed copy available in the archives of
        Canadian Bible College/Canadian Theological
        Seminary, Regina, Saskatchewan, Canada.
TF   *Triumphs of Faith*
WWW   *The Word, the Work and the World*

Albert Benjamin Simpson and the Fourfold Gospel: The Journey of a Spiritual Pilgrim

THE FIGURE OF Albert Benjamin Simpson (1843–1919), though generally neglected by religious historians, nonetheless looms large on the horizon of late nineteenth-century North American evangelicalism. His personal spiritual pilgrimage and multifaceted ministry embodied several of the major currents of spiritual awakening that determined the course of evangelical Protestantism throughout the second half of the nineteenth century. Though the Christian and Missionary Alliance founded by Simpson eventually developed its own denominational agenda, his spiritual pursuits captured the inner yearnings of a sizeable segment of evangelicals in Canada, the United States, and Britain. Consequently, his vision of the Christian life exerted an influence far beyond the borders of his own organization.

The immense breadth of his activity made him a spiritual mentor to a wide range of people who did not formally associate themselves with the Alliance. He was simultaneously a revivalist preacher, a holiness prophet of the "sanctified," "deeper," or "higher Christian life," a commentator on contemporary world events and religious trends, an educational innovator, an author and editor, a poet and hymn writer, an enthusiast for world missions, a theological synthesizer, and an eschatological speculator. Not surprisingly, Simpson's personal spirituality, expressed in the objectives of the organizations he spawned, resonated with many in the modern Pentecostal movement who had sat by and had drunk from the same spiritual streams in which he was refreshed. An appreciation for Simpson as both a devout spiritual seeker and a religious entrepreneur who creatively adapted the structures and ideology of other movements for his own purposes is essential to understanding his posture toward Pentecostalism, which became a catalyst in sensitizing him to new dimensions of spiritual reality.

The motto "Fourfold Gospel" was first coined by Simpson at the outset of the March 1890 convention held at the Gospel Tabernacle in New York City. It was intended to crystallize and convey publicly the distinctive doctrinal convictions of his movement—Christ as Savior, Sanctifier, Healer, and Coming King.[1] Understood in terms of its historical development, the expression provides the interpretative key to understanding the integral relationship between those pivotal crisis religious experiences that energized the spiritual journeys of Simpson and his associates and the statements of faith they formulated. Furthermore, it sheds considerable light on the degree to which Simpson and the Alliance derived their spiritual expectations, theological language, and practical momentum from other transcontinental movements that sought to renew large numbers of Protestants in the United States, British Isles, and western Europe during the closing decades of the nineteenth century.

In his commemorative volume *Twenty-Five Wonderful Years* (1914), which he dedicated to Reverend and Mrs. A. B. Simpson, George Pardington, an early Alliance theologian and historian of Methodist extraction, contextualized the genesis of the organization. He pinpointed its inspirational and theological dependence upon "five providential movements."[2] Pardington concisely identified those nineteenth-century movements "whose Spirit and purpose fused and focused in the Christian and Missionary Alliance" as: (1) gospel evangelism conducted by Charles Finney,

---

[1] On the origin of the phrase "Fourfold Gospel" see "The Opening of the Convention," CAMW 4 (March 7–14, 1890): 157; W. T. MacArthur, *Twenty Sermonettes* (n.p.: published privately, n.d.), 48; Kenneth Mackenzie, "My Memories of Dr. Simpson," AW 72 (July 31, 1937): 485–87, 490, esp. 485. Cf. John Sawin, "The Fourfold Gospel," in *The Birth of a Vision*, ed. David F. Hartzfeld and Charles Nienkirchen (Beaverlodge, Alberta: Buena Books, 1986), 3–6, 18 n. 10.

[2] George Pardington, *Twenty-five Wonderful Years 1889–1914* (New York: Christian Alliance, 1914), 13.

Dwight Moody and Ira Sankey, Major D. Whittle and Philip Bliss; (2) the holiness movement in Europe and America promoted by George Müller, Horatius Bonar, Frances Havergal, Charles Finney, and Dr. Walter and Mrs. Phoebe Palmer; (3) the divine healing movement associated with Dorothea Trüdel (Switzerland), Pastor Johann Blumhardt (Germany), Pastor Otto Stockmayer (Switzerland), William Boardman and Mrs. Elizabeth Baxter (England), Dr. Charles Cullis, Carrie F. Judd, and "Father" Allen (United States); (4) the modern missionary movement heralded by William Carey; and (5) the rebirth of premillennialism embodied in the eschatological teaching of James Brookes (St. Louis) and Adoniram J. Gordon (Boston).[3]

Christ as "Savior": Simpson's Reformed and Puritan Roots

The spiritual journey of Albert Simpson was firmly anchored in the theology and spirituality of the Protestant Reformation, which, though he modified it in later stages of his life, he never relinquished. Born and baptized as an infant into the Scottish Presbyterian tradition on Prince Edward Island in 1843, Simpson described his childhood religious experience as the product of a disciplined father who was "a good Presbyterian of the old school," a doctrinal system derived from the Westminster Shorter Catechism, and a home atmosphere governed by the "conventional rules" of a "well ordered" Puritanism.[4] He recalled a rare boyhood whipping obtained for the violation of his father's strict sabbatarian ethic.[5] Among the Reformed and Puritan classics to which Simpson was exposed during his youth were Thomas Boston's *Human Nature in its Fourfold Estate* (1720); Richard Baxter's *The Saints' Everlasting Rest* (1650); and Philip Doddridge's *The Rise and Progress of Religion in the Soul* (ca. 1745).[6]

---

[3] Ibid., 14–17.

[4] SS, 7. On Simpson's Scottish Presbyterian ancestry and the role of his forefathers in establishing Cavendish on Prince Edward Island, see Harold Simpson, *Cavendish: Its History, Its People, Its Founding Families* (Amherst, Nova Scotia: Harold H. Simpson, n.d.), 28–70, 83–115, 149–66, 238. He was baptized as an infant by Rev. John Geddie, who later distinguished himself as a pioneer Presbyterian missionary to the New Hebrides Islands.

[5] SS, 8.

[6] SS, 7. His mother, Jane Clark, also of Scottish ancestry, was fond of reading old English poets and was the recipient of tales of the Scottish

The earliest impact of this tradition upon Simpson was the cultivation of what he termed "a spirit of reverence and discipline" as well as a "natural horror for evil things." This solidified his moral formation in adult life. Equally beneficial to him was the intensive doctrinal instruction offered by both his home and church. Though by his own admission much of it exceeded his youthful comprehension, it nevertheless constructed a deep reservoir of truth from which he later drew throughout his five decades of public ministry.[7]

Simpson's adolescent conversion in 1858, while residing near Chatham, Ontario, was largely effected through the reading of Walter Marshall's *Gospel Mystery of Salvation* (1692), a seventeenth-century, Scottish Puritan work that according to Alliance scholar Gerald McGraw also "whetted [Simpson's] appetite for holiness and revealed to him some vital principles inherent in sanctification."[8] For Simpson, the discovery of Marshall's admonition to appropriate personally the biblical promises of salvation was a timely corrective to the ultra-predestinarianism of his Presbyterian forebears that "left [him] without any Gospel."[9]

> Marshall became the "voice," absent in Simpson's heritage, that illumined "the simple way of faith" and led him from an "intense and tremendous search for God and eternal life" into a satisfying experience of regeneration with its attendant joyful assurance of the forgiveness of sins.[10]

The seemingly fatalistic "stern theology" of Simpson's native Scottish Presbyterian environment, which prior to his en-

---

Reformation via her maternal grandmother. See A. E. Thompson, A. B. *Simpson. His Life and Work*, rev. ed. (Camp Hill: Christian Publications, 1960), 2, 7, 8.

[7] SS, 8.

[8] Gerald E. McGraw, "The Doctrine of Sanctification in the Published Writings of Albert Benjamin Simpson" (Ph.D. diss., New York University, 1986), 138; cf. Simpson's account in SS, 13, and his extensive quoting of Marshall in *The Cross of Christ* (New York: Alliance Press, 1910), 97–101.

[9] SS, 12.

[10] Ibid., 12, 13. Herbert F. Stevenson in *Keswick's Authentic Voice: Sixty-Five Dynamic Addresses Delivered at the Keswick Convention 1875–1958*, ed. Herbert F. Stevenson (London: Marshall, Morgan and Scott, 1959), 13, simplistically sees Marshall's work as containing all that "Keswick later re-minted in present-day language." His statement ignores the influence of Methodism and the deeper life movement on early Keswick.

countering Marshall had only driven him into a state of spiritual darkness and psychological despondency, was displaced by a doctrine of active faith that enabled him "to receive a new heart and all the gracious operations of the Holy Spirit."[11]

Simpson's teenage commitment to pursue a ministerial vocation also stemmed from his Reformed and Puritan roots. Coincident with his reading of Marshall, Simpson was inspired by Philip Doddridge's *The Rise and Progress of Religion in the Soul* to draw up a covenant with God in which he "gave [himself] wholly to God . . . for every promised blessing, and especially for the grace and power to use [his] life for [God's] service and glory."[12] With minimal modifications, Simpson transcribed Doddridge's covenant, signing his own name instead.[13] Far from abandoning this Puritan covenant-making dimension of his early journey when he later embraced other streams of spirituality, Simpson renewed this covenant as late as 1878.[14]

Despite the vacillations of his life as a theological student at Knox College on the campus of the University of Toronto (1861–65), to which Simpson attributed the "withering" of "the sweetness and preciousness of [his] early piety,"[15] his Reformed and Puritan roots provided the sole framework to this point for the theological interpretation of his spiritual journey. Simpson's years at Knox College predictably prepared him to remain within the Scottish Presbyterian constituency.[16] Nothing in his formal theological education foreshadowed what was to come later in his spiritual development. His impressive academic exploits while

---

[11]SS, 12, 13; cf. Simpson's account of discovering "regeneration" in "Friday Meeting Talks," CMAW 25 (October 13, 1900): 207.

[12]SS, 14.

[13]See Simpson's own words to this effect in "Harvest Home," CMAW 25 (October 20, 1900): 19; compare Simpson's covenant as it appears in Thompson, *Simpson*, 19–22, with Doddridge's in *The Rise and Progress of Religion in the Soul*, A New Edition (Banbury: W. Rusher, 1809), 158–68.

[14]Thompson, *Simpson*, 23.

[15]SS, 18.

[16]Richard Vaudry describes Knox College during the period 1844–61 as having "strong transatlantic ties to its parent church in Scotland" in its role as "an inheritor and transmitter of Scottish theological traditions" ("Theology and Education in Early Victorian Canada: Knox College, Toronto, 1844–1861," *Studies in Religion/Sciences Religieuses* 16 [Fall 1987]: 431–32).

at Knox College included a prize-winning apology for the Presbyterian practice of paedobaptism by sprinkling.[17]

Ordained to the Presbyterian ministry in 1865, Simpson was inducted into his first pastoral charge, Knox Presbyterian Church in Hamilton, Ontario (1865–73).[18] In hindsight he judged his initial experience in professional ministry as "conscientious," "orthodox," and "earnest," but lacking in any knowledge of "the deeper work of the Holy Spirit" and "the life of faith and holiness."[19] Additionally, he depreciated the spiritual depth of his aspirations and methods as pastor of Canada's second largest Presbyterian congregation by likening them to those of a person endeavoring "to build up a successful business."[20] Some evidence does, however, hint at a desire on Simpson's part to move his Hamilton parishioners beyond their conventional church experience. According to church records, in 1871 a decision was made to inaugurate a regular midweek congregational meeting for the fostering of spiritual life.[21]

Christ as "Sanctifier": Deeper Life, Quietist, and Revivalist Phases of the Journey

Ironically, Simpson commenced his second pastorate at Chestnut Street Presbyterian Church in Louisville, Kentucky (1874–79), by announcing to his congregation that he "would not prove to be the apostle of any new revelation or become the exponent of any new truth."[22] However, on the occasion of the sixtieth anniversary of his ordination, which he celebrated in 1915 at Knox Presbyterian Church in Hamilton, Simpson reflected on his dissatisfaction with his inner spiritual condition as a Presbyterian clergyman upon his arrival in Louisville. He reiterated the lengthy, vain struggle "with his own intense nature, his strong self-will, his peculiar temptations" as well as the constant humil-

---

[17]SS, 18–19.

[18]See the full account of his ordination in the *Hamilton Spectator* (September 11, 12, 13, 1865), which differs from Thompson, *Simpson*, 41f.

[19]SS, 21.

[20]Ibid.

[21]See William Campbell, "A History of Knox Presbyterian Church, Hamilton, Ontario" (unpublished typed manuscript, 1967), 12; cf. Thompson, *Simpson*, 50.

[22]As quoted in Thompson, *Simpson*, 53.

iation of his spiritual life that plagued him at that time. The "deeper things of the Spirit" about which he spoke to others lacked personal authentication.[23]

Simpson credited his initiation into the "sanctified," "Spirit-filled," "higher and deeper" life in 1874 to the reading of "an old musty book" on the subject "The Higher Christian Life" he had serendipitously discovered in his library. By his estimation, the personal transformation which ensued was revolutionary, not unlike his conversion experience in 1858:

> As [I] pored over that little volume, [I] saw a new light. The Lord Jesus revealed Himself as a living and all-sufficient presence and [I] learned for the first time that Christ had not saved us from future peril and left us to fight the battle of life as best we could, but He who had justified us was waiting to sanctify us. Across the threshold of [my] Spirit there passed a Being as real as the Christ who came to John on Patmos, and from that moment a new secret has been the charm, and glory, and strength of [my] life and testimony. And [I] shall never forget how [I] longed to come back to the land of [my] birth and the friends of former years, and tell them that magic, marvellous secret, hid from ages and generations, but now made manifest in the saints, which is Christ in you, the Hope of glory.[24]

Simpson's reading of William E. Boardman's *The Higher Christian Life* (1858) marked the beginning of his identification with the spirituality of an interdenominational, transcontinental, higher- and deeper-life movement in which Boardman was a guiding force in both the United States and England.[25] Though largely forgotten in the twentieth century, Boardman's reputation was widespread in the second half of the nineteenth century.[26]

---

[23]Simpson, "A Personal Testimony," AW 45 (October 2, 1915): 11. On the emptiness of Simpson's spiritual life at this point, see also his comments in *The Fullness of Jesus* (New York: Christian Alliance, 1890), 61–67, 81–82.

[24]Simpson, "Personal Testimony," 11. On the supporting evidence for the 1874 date of Simpson's Spirit baptism, see McGraw, "Sanctification," 151f.

[25]See William E. Boardman, *The Higher Christian Life* (Boston: Henry Hoyt, 1858), and the record of Boardman's life by his wife, Mrs. W E. Boardman, *Life and Labors of the Rev. W. E. Boardman* (New York: D. Appleton, 1887). Boardman's own account of his conversion is given in *He That Overcometh: Or a Conquering Gospel* (London: James Nisbet, 1869), 19–47.

[26]On the success of Boardman's efforts at spreading the doctrine of Christian holiness in non-Methodist circles, see Melvin E. Dieter, *The Holiness Revival of the Nineteenth Century* (Metuchen, N.J.: Scarecrow Press,

Herbert Stevenson identified Boardman's *Higher Christian Life* as one of the literary progenitors of the British Keswick movement.[27] The precise extent of Boardman's direct influence on Simpson is difficult to determine, but doubtlessly Boardman's attempted marriage of his Presbyterian background to a quest for sanctification drawn from Wesleyan and Oberlin circles was attractive to Simpson, given both the profundity of the two men's conversions and the similarities in their subsequent journeys. Both were experientially oriented, itinerant churchmen who articulated a nonsystematic, semipopular theology aimed at integrating their Reformed Presbyterian beginnings with later holiness and healing experiences. They then strove to propagate their hybrid ideas in the broadest possible ecclesiastical context.

Some of the specific themes developed by Boardman that noticeably recurred in Simpson's writings include: (1) a critique of the pervasive naturalism of the age that needed to be reversed by a revival of Christian supernaturalism;[28] (2) a restorationist interpretation of church history with its corollary rejection of the cessationist theory regarding spiritual gifts;[29] (3) an analysis of the doctrinal and experiential deficiencies of the Protestant Reformation;[30] (4) an indictment of established churches because of their ignorance and neglect of the apostolic power of the Holy Spirit;[31] (5) a hermeneutical appeal to the life of Christ, the book of Acts, and Old Testament historical metaphors as biblical sup-

---

1980), 56–57. For the Reformed polemic against Boardman during the late nineteenth and early twentieth centuries, see Jacob J. Abbott, "Boardman's Higher Christian Life," *Bibliotheca Sacra* 24 (July 1860): 508–35; Benjamin B. Warfield, *Perfectionism*, ed. Samuel Craig (Philadelphia: Presbyterian and Reformed, 1967), 219f.; and Henry A. Boardman, *"The Higher Life" Doctrine of Sanctification Tried by the Word of God* (Philadelphia: Presbyterian Board of Publication, 1871). Note also a British publisher's attempt to respond to the growing demand for Boardman's book by marketing a severely edited version of the work (reducing the number of pages by almost half): W. E. Boardman, *The Higher Christian Life* (London: Morgan and Chase, 1870).

[27]Stevenson, ed. *Keswick's Voice*, 14.

[28]Boardman, *He That Overcometh*, ix–xii, 207–16.

[29]W. E. Boardman: *The Higher Christian Life* (Edinburgh: Alexander Strahan, 1859), 143f., 208–13; *The Lord That Healeth Thee* (*Jehovah Rophi*) (London: Morgan and Scott, 1881), 26, 52–63, 83f.; *In the Power of the Spirit: Or, Christian Experience in the Light of the Bible*, new ed. (London: Bemrose and Sons, 1883), 1–6; *Gladness in Jesus* (London: Morgan and Scott, 1872), 112f.

[30]Boardman: *Life*, 19f.; *Gladness*, 81.

[31]Boardman: *Life*, 158–59; *Power*, 76f., 91, 119; *He That Overcometh*, 131, 134, 203–4.

port for the doctrine of a Spirit baptism or "second conversion" subsequent to initial regeneration;[32] (6) the theological distinction between regeneration and Spirit baptism;[33] (7) the interchangeable use of numerous terms and expressions as synonyms for Spirit baptism;[34] (8) the Spirit-filled life as having both crisis and process aspects;[35] (9) the importance of "abiding in Christ" as a means of sustaining the Spirit-filled life;[36] (10) the discipline of holy stillness;[37] (11) an exegesis of Romans 7–8 supporting a distinction between Spirit-baptized and merely converted believers;[38] (12) a repudiation of allegations of "perfectionism";[39] (13) advocacy of the doctrine, experience, and method of receiving divine healing;[40] and (14) an endorsement of radical faith ministry.[41] In view of Simpson's indebtedness to and respect for Boardman, he affectionately alluded to the latter as "dear Mr. Boardman [who had] gone to a higher ministry and a sweeter rest," during an address given at the Bethshan Missionary Training Home in London in 1893.[42]

In his discussion of nineteenth-century evangelical revivalism, Arthur T. Pierson, a Presbyterian promoter of the Keswick movement, made a general observation that elucidates another salient motif in Simpson's conception of the sanctified life. He noted that the quest for increased personal holiness that inundated various streams of late nineteenth-century evangelicalism led many to gravitate toward the writings of the mystics. The seventeenth-century Quietist figures Madame Guyon (1648–1717) and Francis Fénelon (1651–1715) were particularly attractive. At the core of Quietist spirituality was the dogmatic insistence

---

[32]Boardman: *Life*, 70–72, 75, 91, 188; *Gladness*, 134–38; *Power*, 30.

[33]See Boardman's illustration of the difference between building and occupying a house as pertinent to regeneration and Spirit baptism (also used by Simpson) in *Power*, 35; cf. 10–18.

[34]Boardman: *Power*, 4f.; *Gladness*, ix–x.

[35]Boardman: *Life*, 125–33; *Power*, 21f.

[36]Boardman: *Power*, 114–23, 210–18.

[37]Boardman, "The First Step of Faith for Deliverance from Sin," *Thy Healer* 4 (1887): 66–68.

[38]Boardman: *Life*, 180–81; *Gladness*, 55–64.

[39]Boardman, *Life*, 37–43.

[40]Boardman, *The Lord That Healeth Thee*, 9–25.

[41]Boardman, *Faith-Work or the Labours of Dr. Cullis in Boston* (London: W. Isbister, 1874).

[42]See Simpson's address, "The Sun of Righteousness," *Thy Healer* (March 1, 1893): 49.

that the voice of God could be heard only in stillness.[43] Like other nineteenth-century holiness counterparts, Simpson did not align himself with all that was part and parcel of Quietism, but he was drawn to Quietist literature.[44] He recommended it as embodying spiritual principles and disciplines necessary for cultivating an interior life devoted to an intimate knowledge of God.[45]

The Alliance founder traced his recognition of the "power of stillness" and appreciation for the discipline of listening prayer to a book entitled *True Peace*, which had been given to him by an unidentified friend sometime during the mid-1870s, presumably after his arrival in Louisville.[46] It comprised chiefly a distillation of Quietist treatises by Guyon, Fénelon, and Molinos. Compiled anonymously by two Quakers, William Backhouse and James Janson, and intentionally designed for popular consumption, this book underwent twelve reprintings between 1813 and 1877.[47]

---

[43]For a succinct scholarly analysis of the rise and demise of Quietism, see Elfrieda Dubois, "Fénelon and Quietism," in *The Study of Spirituality*, ed. Cheslyn Jones, Geoffrey Wainwright, and Edward Yarnold (New York: Oxford University Press, 1986), 408–15.

[44]In his study of the nineteenth-century Methodist Thomas Upham, Darius Salter concluded that Upham (like Simpson) married Quietist mysticism to his holiness theology without surrendering the essentials of his own Protestant theological tradition. See "Thomas Upham and Nineteenth Century Holiness Theology" (Ph.D. diss., Drew University, Madison, N.J., 1983), esp. 196–247; cf. Upham's *Life, Religious Opinions and Experience of Madame Guyon*, new ed. (London: H. R. Allenson, 1905).

[45]See Simpson's editorial reference to "the invaluable writings of Madame Guyon" in LT 6 (July 1906): 385, and his publication of an article, "The Interior Life," by Guyon in LT 6 (July 1906): 421–25. A review of *Meditations from Fénelon* commended the book for its "deeply spiritual character" (CMAW 32 [July 24, 1909]: 288).

[46]A. B. Simpson, "The Power of Stillness," CMAW 33 (October 16, 1909): 37. He first preached the sermon "The Still Small Voice" in January 1895; see CAFMW 14 (January 22, 1895): 57–59, esp. 59. Thus "a score of years ago" when he was given *True Peace* by a "friend" would extend back to the mid-1870s during his Louisville pastorate. A plausible candidate for Simpson's unidentified friend is the elusive "Miss S.," whom he describes in his diary as "full of God—full of faith and power—lifted above all circumstances and dwelling in heavenly places" and "far ahead of us all." See entries in his Louisville/New York diary for November 22, 24, 1879; March 3, 1880, in SS, 150–51, 152, 178.

[47]A *Guide to True Peace or The Excellency of Inward and Spiritual Prayer*, comps. William Backhouse and James Janson (New York: Harper and Brothers, 1946), vii.

The expanded title of the work, A *Guide to True Peace or The Excellency of Inward and Spiritual Prayer*, disclosed its overall contemplative orientation. The substance of some of the chapter titles— "The Spirit of God Dwells in the Heart of Man," "On Mortification," "On Resignation," "On Self-Annihilation," and "On Perfection or the Union of the Soul with God"—located the book within the mainstream of a centuries-old, pre-Protestant, mystical theological tradition. Significantly, Simpson esteemed his entrance into contemplative spirituality via Quietism as "one of the turning points of [his] life."[48] For him, this discovery made possible the experience of "the Sabbath rest of the soul," which he valued as the "sweetest blessing" known to the believer in this life.[49] In his mind, Simpson joined Quietist mysticism with the Puritan notion of soul-rest and its concomitant doctrine of the progressive stages of regeneration.[50] Furthermore, he did not apparently regard the truths gleaned from Catholic Quietists as a subversion of his Protestant Reformation heritage from which he inherited his theology of justification and conversion.[51] In effect he transcended the bitter soteriological disputes of the sixteenth century by synthesizing a classical Protestant view of justification with a more Catholic concept of sanctification. Every facet of first-generation Alliance spirituality testified to the formative influence of the Quietist strains in Simpson's spiritual journey.[52]

---

[48]Simpson, "Stillness," 37; cf. a longer version in his *The Holy Spirit or Power from on High*, 2 vols. (1895; reprint, Harrisburg: Christian Publications, n.d.), 1: 160–64.

[49]Simpson, "Stillness," 37.

[50]See Simpson's appreciation for Thomas Bromley's *The Way to the Sabbath of Rest or, The Soul's Progress in the Work of Regeneration* (London: Giles Calvert, 1655), expressed in his Louisville/New York diary on December 23, 1879, in SS, 160, 162. On Bromley's doctrine of progressive regeneration, see *Sabbath of Rest*, 1, 2.

[51]On Simpson's supplementing of classical Protestant soteriological doctrines with other more Catholic motifs attractive to the age, see William Pitts, "Holiness as Spirituality: The Religious Quest of A. B. Simpson," *Modern Christian Spirituality: Methodological and Historical Essays*, ed. Bradley C. Hanson (Atlanta: Scholars Press, 1990), 231, 247; cf. McGraw, "Sanctification," 397–99, regarding Simpson's de facto "theory of mutual cooperation" and his attempt to strike a balance between Calvinism and Arminianism in arriving at a full understanding of sanctification.

[52]See my article, " 'Deep Calleth Unto Deep': Stillness in Early Alliance Spirituality," *His Dominion* 14 (Summer 1988): 2–22.

A third stream of spirituality that flowed into Simpson's life during his Louisville pastorate originated through his involvement with the American revivalist and evangelistic team of Major Daniel W. Whittle and Philip P. Bliss, who came to Louisville in 1875. A crucial link between Simpson's prior experience of Spirit baptism as the source of new-found spiritual power for personal holiness and public ministry as well as a commitment to aggressive, citywide evangelism was forged through the Whittle and Bliss campaign in which Simpson performed a coordinating role.[53] His transition to nontraditional ministry at this point was a harbinger of the organizations he would later form in 1887—interdenominational agencies committed to the promotion of the deeper life and the evangelization of the world's neglected, lost peoples. During his Louisville sojourn, Simpson's conceptualization of both the content of the gospel and the nature of the professional ministry was radically reshaped. This made inevitable his formal departure from the Presbyterian world that had previously conditioned and guided him. Though this separation would not come officially until 1881, his inner spiritual evolution had already begun to distance him from his ecclesiastical roots.[54] Plausibly, had it not been for the stiff opposition of his wife, Simpson would have entered directly into an independent deeper life and evangelistic ministry upon the termination of his Louisville pastorate.[55]

[53]On Simpson's involvement in the citywide Whittle and Bliss campaign and its progress in 1875, see the *Louisville Courier Journal*, January 3, 1875, p. 4; March 1, p. 4; March 7, p. 1; March 8, p. 4; March 11, p. 4; March 12, p. 4; March 13, p. 4; March 14, p. 3; March 15, p. 4; for further information on Whittle and Bliss, see *Memoirs of Philip P. Bliss*, ed. D. W. Whittle (New York and Chicago: A. S. Barnes, 1877). I concur with McGraw's rejection of the earlier tradition among Alliance scholars that the Whittle and Bliss meetings and not Boardman's *Higher Christian Life* were primarily responsible for his initiation into the sanctified/Spirit-baptized life. See McGraw, "Sanctification," 162–224. On Simpson's fond recollections of Bliss's involvement in the Louisville meetings, see his memorial address delivered in Louisville after Bliss's tragic death, in Whittle, ed. *Memoirs*, 355.

[54]Simpson's Presbyterian background discouraged an active seeking of sanctification. See his reflections on this in "Four-fold Gospel," *Report of the Christian Convention at Old Orchard Beach, Maine, Held July 31 to August 9, 1887*, supplementary, 20–21. On the conflict between Simpson and his Louisville congregational leaders over a church building program that led to his resignation from the Chestnut Street Presbyterian Church, see Thompson, *Simpson*, 57f.

[55]The intensity of the dispute between Simpson and his wife

Christ as "Healer": Spokesperson for a Movement

The year 1881 brought to a traumatic climax Simpson's process of separation from the Presbyterian Church. Within a space of three months (August–November) he was "miraculously" healed of a chronic heart disorder during a vacation at Old Orchard Beach, Maine, and was baptized by immersion in a Baptist chapel in New York City. These two events culminated in his resignation as pastor of Thirteenth Street Presbyterian Church to commence independent evangelistic outreach among the unchurched poor in New York City.[56] In February 1882, Simpson organized what became the Gospel Tabernacle Church, and within a few months he began Friday afternoon meetings for consecration and healing.[57]

Simpson's involvement with the American faith-healing movement, precipitated by his own professed supernatural cure at Old Orchard Beach in 1881, both intensified the interdenominational direction of his life and solidified what became the third "fold" of his Fourfold Gospel. Central to his interest in faith healing (he preferred the expression "divine healing") was his contact with Charles Cullis, an Episcopalian homeopathic physician from Boston who after 1860 had established a family of institutions that endeavored to propagate holiness and healing doctrines alongside medical relief and foreign missions. Strategically, Cullis was also the dominant figure associated with the

---

flows into the entries for November 10, 17, 22, 25, 27; December 4, 6, 1879, in his Louisville/New York diary, in SS, 149–57. Cf. Simpson's comment on November 10, 1879 (the evening his pastorate was dissolved), that he was now "Christ's free servant" (ibid., 149). Note also his uncertainty over being installed as pastor of the Thirteenth Street Presbyterian Church in New York as opposed to the strength of his vision for a missionary magazine in his diary entries for November 23, 25; December 8, 9, 11, 12, 17, 26, 1879, in SS, 151f.

[56]For an assortment of primary sources confirming Simpson's twofold reason for his resignation—that is, his refusal to continue the practice of infant baptism and his desire for evangelizing the unchurched—see SS, 186–95; on the resistance of the congregation to his vision, see Thompson, *Simpson*, 83f. For Simpson's description of his adult baptism and its meaning to him, see "Baptism, and the Baptism of the Holy Spirit," CMAW 28 (May 17, 1902): 286f.

[57]*Fifty Golden Years* 1882–1932 (New York: Gospel Tabernacle, 1932), 3, 15.

"faith convention" at the Old Orchard camp meeting grounds on the Maine coast.[58]

While attending Cullis's meetings, Simpson was aroused as to the possibility of being divinely cured of debilitating health problems, which had dogged him since adolescence and throughout his various pastorates.[59] He had hitherto sought relief through allopathy and homeopathy.[60] Under Cullis's influence, however, Simpson came to embrace the doctrine that physical healing was a benefit of salvation and could be received by faith. This novel interpretation of Scripture was experientially validated by his subsequent healing, which occurred during an ascent of Mount Kearsarge near Intervale, New Hampshire.[61] From that time on divine healing became an essential component of Simpson's private life and public ministry and was enshrined in the ideological commitments of his deeper-life and missionary organizations.[62]

Borrowing the "healing home" model developed previously by others such as Trüdel, Blumhardt, Boardman, and Judd (Montgomery), Simpson opened his first healing home in his

---

[58]For a survey of Cullis's spiritual journey and work, see Donald W. Dayton, *Theological Roots of Pentecostalism* (Peabody, Mass.: Hendrickson, reprint, 1991), 122–24; Norris Magnuson, *Salvation in the Slums: Evangelical Social Work 1865–1920* (1977; reprint, Grand Rapids: Baker, 1990), 68–70; cf. Cullis's chapter, "A Call to the Hills," in *Intervale Park, Intervale*, N.H. (Boston: Willard Tract Repository, 1886), 11–20; the memorial edition of his periodical *Times of Refreshing* (August 1892); and W. E. Boardman, *Faith-Work*.

[59]On the contact between Simpson and Cullis at Old Orchard Beach, see Simpson, *The Gospel of Healing*, rev. ed. (Harrisburg: Christian Publications, 1915; original ed. 1887), 157–63, esp. 162; cf. his reference to Cullis's meeting in 1881 and his healing at Old Orchard in his "Opening Address," WWW 7 (September 1886): 130. Wm. T. MacArthur, *Twenty Sermonettes*, 47, also graphically describes Simpson's interaction with the faith-healing doctrine at Old Orchard.

[60]See his testimony in *My Medicine Chest or Helps to Divine Healing* (New York: Christian Alliance, 1913), 1; cf. idem, "The Sun of Righteousness," *Thy Healer* (March 1, 1893): 57; idem, "Himself," *Thy Healer* 2 (1885): 233, for a chronicling of his physical ailments.

[61]Simpson, *Healing*, 163–67; cf. "Himself," WWW 5 (October 1885): 288–61.

[62]On the healing of his daughter Margaret, see Simpson, *Healing*, 174–75; regarding his testimonies to his healing given at the Congregational Church in Intervale, New Hampshire, Thirteenth Street Presbyterian Church in New York, and the Fulton Street Prayer Meeting, see ibid., 164, 173–74. The first annual report of the Alliance underscored its commitment "to preach a full Gospel at home and send missionaries to carry the same glad tidings to the unevangelized regions beyond" (AR [1897–98]: 72).

private residence in 1883, which became the forerunner of the Alliance's Berachah Home.[63] During 1884 and 1885 he embarked on a convention tour of eastern American cities. This in turn led to summer camp meetings in various states. At all of these extended gatherings divine healing assumed a prominent place in the program. Thus Simpson was thrust into the limelight of the faith-healing movement in America.[64]

The internationalization of Simpson's reputation as spokesperson for the faith-healing movement was the consequence of his involvement in an International Convention on Holiness and Divine Healing held at Bethshan, London, in 1885, which was attended by delegates from Australia, America, the British Isles, and Europe.[65] The stage was set at the conference for Simpson's rise to prominence by the unexpected absence of higher profile American and European leaders such as Cullis, Judd, Mahan, Stanton, Blumhardt, Zeller, and Stockmayer.[66] His expectations regarding the conference were expressed in the 1885 British edition of his *Gospel of Healing*:

> May God grant that the Conference in London, which assembles just as these pages come from the press, may shed upon these precious truths a marvellous light, and send them forth with new and living power to quicken and comfort the people

---

[63]See Thompson, *Simpson*, 140–43; cf. *The Story of the Christian and Missionary Alliance* (Nyack, N.Y.: Alliance Press, 1900), 22–24.

[64]In view of Simpson's prominent role, it is unfortunate that Paul Chappel gives only minimal attention to him in his survey of the international healing movement of the nineteenth century. See "Origins of the Divine Healing Movement in America," *Spiritus* 1 (Winter 1985): 5–18. Contrarily, Donald W. Dayton ranks Simpson as "second only to Charles Cullis as a leader of the growing Faith Cure movement." See Dayton, *Pentecostalism*, 128; idem, "The Rise of the Evangelical Healing Movement in Nineteenth Century America," *Pneuma* 4 (Spring 1982): 1–18. More generally, see Raymond Cunningham, "From Holiness to Healing: The Faith Cure in America, 1872–1892," *Church History* 43 (December 1974): 499–513.

[65]See W. E. Boardman's call for such a conference in *Record of the International Conference on Divine Healing and True Holiness Held at the Agricultural Hall, London, June 1–5, 1885* (London: J. Snow and Co.; Bethshan, 1885), iv–v; and idem, *Thy Healer* 2 (1885): 14–15, 70.

[66]Concerning the international response to the invitation, see Boardman in *Record*, v, vi; *Thy Healer* 2 (1885): 181–82. The large numbers in attendance caused the conference to be moved from Bethshan to St. Mary's Agricultural Hall. See the advertisement in the *Times*, June 5, 1885, 13.

of God, arouse the church, evangelize the world and hasten the Master's coming.[67]

During the informally conducted sessions, cohosted by W. E. Boardman and Mrs. Elizabeth Baxter, Simpson spoke several times. He identified himself unequivocally with the American faith-healing movement, showed himself in sympathy with nineteenth-century restorationist sentiments, and recounted his own healing.[68] In his celebrated extemporaneous sermon on sanctification and healing entitled "Himself," Simpson articulated a theological position that differed from Wesleyan and Keswickian views, both of which were represented at the conference.[69] The exposure of European adherents of the holiness and healing movement to Simpson was further enhanced by the publication of portions of his *Gospel of Healing* in Bethshan's periodical, *Thy Healer* (1885).[70] Subsequent to the Bethshan Conference, Simpson participated in other similar gatherings conducted throughout England and Scotland.[71] The awareness of being aligned with an international movement providentially raised up to restore holiness and healing to the church, which Simpson absorbed from the Bethshan Conference, stimulated him to solicit European support for a similar venture in the United States, where holiness and healing advocates were still regionalized and lacking a corporate consciousness. Upon his return to New York he called for the

---

[67]A. B. Simpson, *The Gospel of Healing* (London: John Snow, 1885), 7.

[68]For the verbatim text of Simpson's addresses, see *Record*, 38–41, 64–69, 80–86, 126–29, 160–61.

[69]The impromptu sermon was first published by Elizabeth Baxter in *Thy Healer* 2 (1885): 229–34, and later by Simpson in WWW 5 (October 1885): 258–61. It was the inspiration for his hymn "Himself," which was included in every edition of *Hymns of the Christian Life* from 1891 to the present (except the 1897 edition). On Simpson's theology of holiness, see Alliance historian John Sawin's reference to Simpson's "habitationism" in contradistinction to the "suppressionism" of Keswick and the "eradicationism" of the Wesleyan tradition (*Birth of a Vision*, 21). For Simpson, the Alliance doctrine of sanctification was "neither Wesleyan nor strictly speaking, an echo of even the excellent teaching given at . . . Keswick" ("Editorial," CMAW 28 [June 3, 1899]: 8).

[70]See *Thy Healer* 2 (1885): 9–11, 22–25, 32–35, 52–53, 64–66, 79–81, 87–90.

[71]Thompson, *Simpson*, 112–13; cf. *Thy Healer* 2 (1885): 217–19, for Simpson's address at the Liverpool Conference.

formation of a Christian Alliance of all those who held to the "gospel of full salvation."[72]

While his preaching of divine healing was professedly subordinated to the first two "folds" of his Fourfold Gospel, salvation and sanctification, Simpson's presence at Bethshan and his reputation as a disseminator of holiness and healing doctrines alienated him from more conservative evangelicals on both sides of the Atlantic.[73] The British religious periodical *Word and Work* proscribed W. E. Boardman (and by implication Simpson) as "the high priest of [a] new faction" and discredited the Bethshan Conference as an assembly of "neophytes" deluded by "irrational" and "unscriptural" doctrines, devoid of any legitimate ecclesiastical authority to anoint with oil for healing.[74] A more moderate but critical voice, *The Christian*, reprinted a chapter from Simpson's *Gospel of Healing* and accused him of devaluing the importance of the future redemption of the body.[75] Simpson countered that he did

> not deny the still greater work of the Divine Spirit upon the soul, nor should any physical blessing ever receive, a disproportionate place in the symmetrical fulness of the glorious Gospel. As a Christian pastor, God has never allowed me to

---

[72]See Simpson's appeal in *Record*, 160–61, and his summons to form a Christian Alliance in "Editorial," WWW 5 (October 1885): 280.

[73]While recognizing the healing doctrine as "becoming one of the touchstones of character and spiritual life in all the churches of America, and revolutionizing the whole Christian life of thousands," Simpson insisted it was "not the whole gospel, nor perhaps the chief part of it" and needed to "be ever held in its true place in relation to the other parts of the gospel" (*Healing*, 6).

[74]"A New Cult," *Word and Work* 11 (June 18, 1885): 385; "Faith-Healing Today," *Word and Work* 11 (June 18, 1885): 384. The polemic against healing and holiness doctrines continued in "Faith and Failure"; "Health and Holiness," *Word and Work* 11 (June 25, 1885): 400–401, and "Faith-Healing Once More"; "Faith-Healing Failures"; "Medical Faith-Healing"; "Correspondence," *Word and Work* 11 (July 9, 1885): 445–47, 459.

[75]See "Holiness and Healing"; "The Principles of Faith-Healing," *The Christian* (June 11, 1885): 425, 430–31; cf. "Mr. Simpson's Article," *The Christian* (June 18, 1885): 445. The editor attempted to differentiate between Trüdel and Blumhardt, the European pioneers of the movement, whom he commended as "divinely accredited healers" and the more dubious "faith-healing teachers" associated with Bethshan ("The Prayer of Faith," *The Christian* [July 2, 1885]: 483). Cf. the fear and suspicion of the Bethshan conference as an "exhibition of miracles" in an age of exhibitions, while not impugning the motives of the organizers, in "Faith-Healing," *The Record* (June 12, 1885): 589.

stand before his church and the world to be the special advocate of mere physical healing. What we do plead for is a full Gospel, without mutilation, disproportion, defect, or extravagance.[76]

British critics of Simpson's doctrine of divine healing also included persons who would otherwise have heartily applauded his missionary zeal. Mrs. H. Grattan Guinness, whose husband founded the East London Institute for Home and Foreign Missions in 1872 (a model for Simpson's Nyack Missionary Training Institute), blamed the "notorious Dr. Simpson" for the tragic deaths in 1890 of three young missionaries associated with the Kansas Mission to the Soudan [sic]. She charged him with indoctrinating them with his anti-medicine beliefs.[77] Her strident critique of Simpson's *Gospel of Healing* concluded with the warning that

> Dr. Simpson at any rate is not a guide for Christian people to follow. We have surely said enough to show that he teaches foolish, false and very mischievous doctrines; that he is himself the victim of gross delusion, and that his practical counsels are misleading and dangerous.[78]

From within the early twentieth-century Keswick tradition, Griffith Thomas and Herbert Lockyer criticized Simpson's allegedly extreme notion of healing in the atonement as reconcilable with neither Scripture nor his own experience.[79] Roland Bingham, the founder of the Sudan Interior Mission, went to great lengths to expose the glaring inconsistencies between Simpson's faith-healing doctrine, the purported manner in which Simpson

---

[76]See Simpson's "Letter to the Editor," *The Christian* (June 25, 1885): 478. More objective reporting on the Bethshan conference appeared in the secular press. For example, see "Modern Miracles," *The Daily Telegraph*, June 5, 1885, 3; and "Modern Miracles," *The Daily Telegraph*, June 6, 1885, 3.

[77]See Mrs. H. Grattan Guinness: "The Kansas Soudan Mission," *Regions Beyond* (September/October 1890): 378; "Faith-Healing and Missions," *Regions Beyond* (November 1890): 411; "Faith-Healing and Missions," *Regions Beyond* (December 1890): 466; "Faith-Healing and Missions," *Regions Beyond* (January 1891): 24.

[78]Guinness, "Faith-Healing and Missions," *Regions Beyond* (January 1891): 24–32, esp. 32.

[79]See Griffith Thomas's introduction to Rowland V. Bingham, *The Bible and the Body* (1921; reprint, London and Edinburgh: Marshall, Morgan and Scott, 1939), vii; Herbert Lockyer, *The Healer and Healing Movements* (Stirling, Scotland: Drummond's Tract Depot, 1935), 10, 14–18, 22.

died, and the ongoing practice of his followers with regard to the use of medicine.[80]

Simpson remained undaunted in the face of evangelical criticism. Prior to and following the Bethshan Conference he repeatedly championed the cause of faith healing in response to the opposition of other religious critics, including the Presbyterian clergy of New York to which he had once belonged.[81] At the risk of losing his "orthodox" image and ministerial credibility in established churches, he chose to hold resolutely to his conviction regarding divine healing, though not without some modification.[82] Moreover, he retained his relationships with those in the holiness and healing movement whose views bordered on eccentricity.[83] Ironically, it was Simpson's avowed commitment to a proportionate emphasis on divine healing under the rubric of his Fourfold Gospel that earned him verbal abuse from John A. Dowie, the infamous healing evangelist who founded Zion City, Illinois. Chagrined by Simpson's refusal to accompany him on a cross-country healing campaign, sometime prior to 1885, Dowie maligned him as a fraud and betrayer of divine healing.[84]

---

[80]Bingham, Bible, 19–20, 53–54, 96–103,

[81]See Simpson's response to Dr. Hepworth's criticism of faith healing in "Editorial," WWW 1 (November 1882): 261; his reply to adverse criticism in the Independent, in "Editorial," WWW 1 (December 1882): 327; the reaction of the New York Presbyterian clergy to faith healing in "Editorial," WWW 5 (January 1885): 31, and his rejoinder to a Sunday School Times article against divine healing in "Editorial," WWW 5 (December 1885): 348–49.

[82]For a careful analysis of the changes in Simpson's views on healing, see David M. Pett, "Divine Healing: The Development of Simpson's Thought," His Dominion 16 (1, 1989): 23–33.

[83]See Simpson's collaboration with Captain R. Kelso Carter, a healing extremist who later revised his views, in the first edition of his Hymns of The Christian Life ed. Captain R. Kelso Carter and Rev. A. B. Simpson (New York: Christian Alliance, 1891).

[84]A. W. Tozer, Wingspread (Harrisburg: Christian Publications, 1943), 134–35, does not date the incident, but sometime prior to Simpson's six-city tour of 1885 is probable. For examples of Dowie's invective against Simpson, the Christian Alliance, and Captain R. Kelso Carter, see John Alexander Dowie: "The Great Neglected Chapter," Leaves of Healing 3 (September 25, 1897): 763–67; "The Great Neglected Chapter," Leaves of Healing 4 (March 12, 1898): 388–90, 391, 392, 393. On the other hand, after cataloging Dowie's numerous vices, Simpson dismissed him as a "misguided" man who gave "undue pre-eminence" to divine healing ("Collapse of Dowieism," LT 6 [June 1906]: 327–28). For a crisp survey of Dowie's rise to prominence, see Edith L. Blumhofer, "The Christian Catholic Apostolic Church and the Apostolic Faith: A Study in the 1906 Pentecostal Revival,"

The whole of Simpson's post-1881 career demonstrates an effort to prevent the undue elevation of healing above his foremost concerns of evangelizing lost souls and promoting the Spirit-filled life. Nevertheless, healing was the vehicle through which hundreds found their way into the early Alliance, including many of Simpson's most gifted leaders.[85]

Christ as "Coming King": The Development of Eschatological Consciousness

The animating force in Simpson's Alliance was generated by the eschatological fourth "fold" of his Fourfold Gospel. Again events in Simpson's own life were pivotal. In an article entitled "How I was Led to Believe in Premillenarianism," published in 1891, he related that during the late 1870s he had abandoned the spiritualized, a/post-millennial interpretation of Christ's coming that he had imbibed during his seminary days and taught during his first two pastorates.[86] While Simpson attributed his conversion to premillennialism to "new light . . . thrown upon the Word" by the Holy Spirit, it was more than coincidental that his discarding of the "old [prophetic] axioms" of his professors in favor of the revived premillennial doctrine of an imminent personal reign of Christ was concurrent with a blossoming of premillennial fervor among American evangelicals during the latter half of the nineteenth century.[87] A general interest in prophecy and the literal interpretation of events "predicted" in the Bible gained sufficient momentum to give birth to a burgeoning prophecy conference movement. The First International Prophetic Conference convened in New York City in 1878, the year before Simpson's arrival.[88]

---

in *Charismatic Experiences in History*, ed. Cecil M. Robeck, Jr. (Peabody, Mass.: Hendrickson, 1985), 126–46.

[85]See the collection of Alliance leaders' healing testimonies in *A Cloud of Witnesses Concerning Divine Healing*, ed. A. B. Simpson (New York: Word, Work and World, 1887); *Modern Miracles*, ed. David J. Fant, Jr. (Harrisburg: Christian Publications, 1943).

[86]Simpson, "How I was Led to Believe in Premillenarianism," CAMW 7 (November 13, 1891): 298.

[87]Regarding the exchange of Anglo and American millenarian ideas after 1848, see Ernest Sandeen, *The Roots of Fundamentalism* (Chicago: University of Chicago Press, 1970), 57–58.

[88]See *Premillennial Essays of the Prophetic Conference Held in the Church*

Simpson was but one of many prominent evangelical pastors, including James H. Brookes of St. Louis, Adoniram J. Gordon of Boston, Cyrus I. Scofield of Dallas, Arthur T. Pierson and W. J. Erdman (Pierson and Erdman served multiple Presbyterian pastorates), who fed their congregations a full diet of premillennialism during the 1880s and 1890s. In addition, the most notable itinerant evangelists of the day—D. L. Moody, Major D. W. Whittle, Reuben A. Torrey, and Billy Sunday—were also numbered among the ranks of the premillennialists.[89] Though essentially a historicist in his interpretation of the book of Revelation, Simpson also displayed some sympathy for dispensational thought, as shown by his participation in a convention sponsored by C. I. Scofield's Congregational Church in 1892.[90] A thorough comparison of the major prophetic works of Simpson and those of H. Grattan Guinness, the English evangelist and Fellow of the Royal Astronomical Society who was involved in Simpson's 1858 conversion[91] and provided the philosophy and structure for his Missionary Training Institute,[92] shows numerous substantive

---

of the Holy Trinity, New York City, ed. Nathaniel West (New York: Revell, 1879). Cf. Simpson's reference to the revival of premillennialism and his refutation of postmillennialism in The Gospel of the Kingdom (New York: Christian Alliance, 1890), 13–14, 23f.

[89]Timothy P. Weber lists the various nineteenth-century proponents of premillennial theory in Living in the Shadow of the Second Coming (Chicago: University of Chicago Press, 1987), 32–33.

[90]Simpson's historicist and dispensationalist inclinations are discussed by Franklin Pyles in "The Missionary Eschatology of A. B. Simpson," in Birth of a Vision, 30–35.

[91]See Thompson, Simpson, 26.

[92]On Guinness's involvement in the establishment of Missionary Training Schools in the United States during the 1880s, see Henry C. Mabie, "A Plea For Missionary Institutes," Regions Beyond (February 1890): 51–56, esp. 51, 52; cf. Guinness, "The Training of Missionaries," Regions Beyond (August 1888): 232–37; Part 2, ibid. (September/October 1888): 262–68. The philosophy, objectives, and structure of Guinness's Institute, explained in Mrs. H. Grattan Guinness, The Wide World and Our Work in It (London: Hodder and Stoughton, 1886), were almost identical to Simpson's Missionary Training Institute. Compare Simpson, "New York Missionary Training College," WWW 5 (October 1885): 270–72. Both schools were conceived in eschatological consciousness. The Guinnesses included appendixes on their institute in two of their prophetic volumes; see H. Grattan Guinness, The Approaching End of the Age Viewed in the Light of History, Prophecy, and Science (1878; reprint, London: Hodder and Stoughton, 1882), 694–98; and Mr. and Mrs. H. Grattan Guinness, The Divine Programme of the World's History (London: Hodder and Stoughton, 1888), 451–55.

similarities. Among many indications of Guinness's influence is Simpson's use of "lunar," "solar," and "calendar" time in constructing prophetic chronologies.[93] Furthermore, the Bethshan circle with which Simpson came in direct contact in 1885 was also a hotbed for premillennial speculation.[94] On the American side, A. J. Gordon of Boston was Simpson's primary eschatological mentor.[95]

None provided a better late nineteenth-century illustration of the intricate connection between premillennialism and an aggressive missionary program than Simpson and the Alliance.

While still in his New York Presbyterian pastorate, Simpson undertook the publication of *The Gospel in All Lands*, the first illustrated missionary magazine in North America (1880).[96] He

---

[93]Compare Simpson, *The Gospel of the Kingdom*, 221f., and Mr. and Mrs. H. Grattan Guinness, *Light for the Last Days* (London: Hodder and Stoughton, 1886), 219–32, 233–47, 248–68, 648–71. Both volumes had foldout, prophetic charts attached inside the front covers; cf. H. Grattan Guinness, *Approaching End of the Age*, 388–460, 509–674, for his elaborate astronomical schemes for measuring prophetic time. Simpson published several articles by Guinness in his magazine, respectful of the latter's established reputation as a defender of premillennialism. See, for example, Guinness: "The Coming of Christ a Stimulus to Missionary Zeal," CAFMW 17 (October 2, 1896): 306–7; "Surely, I Come Quickly," CAFMW 15 (December 1895): 375. In a British context, see Mr. and Mrs. H. Grattan Guinness, "The Second Coming: Will It Be Before the Millennium?" *The British Weekly* 34 (June 24, 1887): 113–15; Part 2, ibid. (July 1, 1887): 130–31. Other pertinent prophetic works by Guinness include: *Key to the Apocalypse* (London: Hodder and Stoughton, 1899); *Romanism and the Reformation from the Standpoint of Prophecy* (London: Hodder and Stoughton, 1887); and *History Unveiling* (London and Edinburgh: Revell, 1905). Numerous themes parallel those found in Simpson's other major prophetic volumes: *The Coming One* (New York: Christian Alliance, 1912); *Back to Patmos* (New York: Christian Alliance, 1914); and *Heaven Opened* (New York: Alliance Press, 1899).

[94]Rev. Michael Baxter, the husband of Elizabeth Baxter who cofounded the Bethshan healing home, edited *Signs of Our Time* (1872–75), a monthly magazine which published numerous articles of a historical, premillennial persuasion and indulged in rabid date setting.

[95]In his eulogy of Gordon, Simpson described him as "one of the truest friends of our work" and assessed Gordon's premillennial volume, *Ecce Venit: Behold He Cometh* (New York: Revell, 1889), as "one of the best ever published on that theme." See also Simpson, "Rev. A. J. Gordon," CAFMW 14 (February 12, 1895): 97–102. Gordon was also a contributor to Simpson's magazine. See his article, "Latter Day Delusions," WWW 7 (November 1886): 296–309.

[96]See Simpson's reference to starting *The Gospel in All Lands* in 1880, in "Mission Work," *Report of the Christian Convention at Old Orchard Beach,*

editorialized that the evangelization of the world was "the great unfulfilled condition of the Lord's return."[97] Simpson was apparently the only nineteenth-century evangelical leader to assert the evangelization of the world as a precondition to Christ's second advent.[98] The American Protestant Zionist William E. Blackstone delivered a signal address on "The Need of the World and the Work of the Church" at Old Orchard in 1886, which induced Simpson to organize his deeper life and missionary fraternities, the Evangelical Missionary Alliance and the Christian Alliance, the following year.[99] Blackstone's premillennially charged pleas for North American Christians to sacrifice themselves for the sake of the overseas missionary enterprise harmonized perfectly with Simpson's platform. He was a fitting early vice-president of the Christian and Missionary Alliance and a frequent speaker at Simpson's conventions.[100] Furthermore, his persistent lobbying on behalf of Jewish immigration to Palestine found ready sympathy in Alliance circles.[101] A stated objective of the Christian Alli-

---

Maine, Held July 31st to August 9th, 1887 (New York: Word, Work and World, 1887), 108; cf. SS, 154.

[97]Simpson, "Editorial," *The Gospel in All Lands* 1 (February 1880): 60.

[98]For other evidence of this connection, see Simpson: "Editorial," WWW 3 (March 1883): 47; "Editorial," CAFMW 12 (February 16, 1894): 169.

[99]See W. E. Blackstone, "The Need of the World and the Work of the World," WWW 7 (September 1886): 132–37. For the deep impression Blackstone's address left on Simpson, see his later reference to it in "Editorial," WWW 7 (December 1886): 374–75; and again twenty-five years later in his annual report for 1913–14 [AR (1913–14): 3].

[100]See the notation in AW 35 (January 28, 1911): 287. Blackstone was best known for his premillennial manifesto, *Jesus is Coming* (1898; reprint, New York: Revell, 1932). A chapter by Blackstone entitled "God's Dealing with the Nations" was included in Philip Mauro, et al., *The Signs of the Times* (New York: Alliance Press, 1907), 29–51.

[101] In 1891 Blackstone submitted to American President Benjamin Harrison a petition signed by 413 Christian and Jewish leaders supporting the right of Jews to return to Palestine. See *Palestine for the Jews: A Copy of the Memorial presented to President Harrison March 5*, 1891 (n.p.: 1891); cf. Simpson's editorial, "Zionism and the Jews," CMAW 25 (August 18, 1900): 89, in which he links Zionism and the reorganization of the Jewish state to the fulfillment of prophecy and his strong pro-Zionist sentiments expressed in *Larger Outlooks on Missionary Lands* (New York: Christian Alliance, 1893), 64–65, 96–101; idem, *A Great Missionary Movement* (New York: Christian Alliance, 1892), 43–46. The first annual report of the Christian and Missionary Alliance (1897–98) urged a "renewed diligence to prayer and the work of sending the Gospel to the Jews that they may be speedily established in their own land" (AR [1897–98], 89).

ance was to "promote the wide diffusion" of "Christ's personal and premillennial coming" along with the other "folds" of the gospel.[102]

Apparently, Simpson did not go so far as to impose premillennialism as a criterion for fellowship in the Alliance, as he did with salvation, sanctification, and healing.[103] This tolerance of eschatological viewpoints that he extended to his co-workers, however, did not diminish the intensity of his own end-time sense of urgency to fulfill the church's missionary mandate. His presidential address in 1915 concluded with an announcement of the impending climax of human history, no doubt underscored by the recent outbreak of World War I. He summoned the Alliance council to be mindful of the prophetic calendar:

> The solemn and eventful times amid which we meet call us to "be not unwise, but understanding what the will of the Lord is, redeeming the time because the days are evil." The things which we have long expected from the study of the prophetic Word at last appear to be gathering fast and bringing near the crisis of the age. It is a time of worldwide opportunity, wonderful privilege, and sacred responsibility. Upon us "the ends of the age have come," and the Master may be sending us forth as the last heralds of His Kingdom and His coming. We seem to hear the midnight cry, "Behold the Bridegroom cometh!" Shall we from this Council with new earnest, and faith and hope go out to meet Him?[104]

Simpson's adherence to the premillennial cause undergirded his restorationist ideology (discussed in ch. 3), which saw the history of the church after two millennia as ending where it began—with the proclamation of the "full gospel" known to Christ

---

[102] See the constitution of the Christian Alliance in WWW 9 (August and September 1887): 110–11, esp. 110. In May 1887, Simpson advertised the Convention at Old Orchard as "The Christian Convention for Christian Teaching, Life and Work and Foreign Missions," in his "Editorial," WWW 8 (May 1887): 317. He promised to organize more fully the missionary movement begun the preceding summer at Old Orchard.

[103] See WWW 9 (August and September 1887): 111. Neither was premillennialism explicitly stated in the constitution of the Evangelical Missionary Alliance, which Simpson also founded in 1887. See WWW 9 (August and September 1887): 111–12; for a similar tendency, cf. the constitution of Simpson's International Missionary Alliance (1892) in Missionary Movement, 33–34.

[104] "Annual Report of the President and General Superintendent of the Christian and Missionary Alliance," AR (1914–15): 28.

and the apostles. In his espousal of restorationist ideals he simply shared with eighteenth- and nineteenth-century Baptists, evangelical Episcopalians, Churches of Christ, a variety of holiness groups, and Mormons what David Edwin Harrell, Jr., has termed perhaps "the most vital single assumption underlying the development of American Protestantism."[105] The restorationist banner was most dramatically carried into the twentieth century by Pentecostals, who claimed merely to continue in their quest for primitive Christianity where Simpson and others had stopped.[106]

---

[105]As quoted in Richard T. Hughes, "Introduction: On Recovering the Theme of Recovery," in *The American Quest for the Primitive Church*, ed. Richard T. Hughes (Urbana and Chicago: University of Illinois Press, 1988), 7. On the importance and varying concepts of restorationism and restitutionism in eighteenth-, nineteenth-, and twentieth-century American religious life, see the collection of essays in *The American Quest*, ed. Richard T. Hughes; and Samuel S. Hill, Jr., "A Typology of American Restitutionism: From Frontier Revivalism and Mormonism to the Jesus Movement," *Journal of the American Academy of Religion* 44 (March 1976): 65–76.

[106] See Grant Wacker, "Playing for Keeps: The Primitivist Impulse in Early Pentecostalism," in *The American Quest*, 196–219.

THE PENTECOSTAL "DEBT" TO SIMPSON AND THE EARLY ALLIANCE

AS PENTECOSTAL SCHOLARSHIP has matured in the twentieth century, the indebtedness of modern Pentecostalism to its historical anteced-ents has been increasingly acknowledged by historians. Second-generation Pentecostal historiography, like the first generation of Pentecostal pioneers, recognizes that twentieth-century Pentecos-talism, which was born as an international movement in the cradle of Azusa Street (1906–13), stands on the shoulders of those spiri-tual giants of the late nineteenth century who awakened large numbers of people in America and western Europe to the possi-bility of heightened levels of Christian experience through the power of the Holy Spirit.[1]

Pentecostal Assessments of Simpson and the Early Alliance

With virtual unanimity, historians of several Pentecostal traditions have given generous tribute to the seminal contribu-

---

[1] For a survey of the debate among Pentecostal scholars over the precise historical significance of Azusa Street, see Cecil M. Robeck, Jr., "The International Significance of Azusa Street," *Pneuma* 8 (Spring 1986): 1–4; cf. J. R. Goff, Jr.'s thesis, which identifies Charles Parham as the founder of the Pentecostal movement, summarized in his article "Parham, Charles Fox (1873–1929)," DPCM, 660–61.

tion made by Simpson and the Alliance to the genesis and development of the modern Pentecostal movement during its infant and adolescent stages.

Donald Gee, the astute British Pentecostal leader, credited Simpson with originating the "Fourfold Gospel" and observed that Pentecostals subsequently modified it for their own use by substituting the baptism of the Holy Spirit for sanctification.[2] He bemoaned the lack of attention given to holy living in the Pentecostal assemblies and preferred to have "a Fivefold Gospel [with] sanctification [to] a Fourfold Gospel without it."[3] Reflecting on the nineteenth century, Gee assessed the "saintly A. B. Simpson" as having had a ministry in North America parallel to that of R. A. Torrey, whose preaching of the baptism of the Spirit sowed the seeds of the Pentecostal movement in Germany.[4]

Oral Roberts University professor Steve Durasoff interpreted Simpson's "distinct and convincing emphasis on divine healing" as part and parcel of a "season of deep spiritual searching which immediately preceded the twentieth-century Pentecostal revival."[5] Vinson Synan, a Pentecostal Holiness Church historian, numbered Simpson (along with R. A. Torrey and Andrew Murray) among those who by virtue of their emphasis on the need for all believers to experience a personal Pentecost were responsible for "[setting] . . . the stage . . . for the rise of the modern Pentecostal movement."[6] AG historian Carl Brumback asserted that the legacy of Simpson to Pentecostalism was pervasive.[7] It included the following: (1) doctrines borrowed from the Alliance;[8]

---

[2] Donald Gee, *Now That You've Been Baptized in the Spirit* (1930; reprint, Springfield, Mo.: Gospel Publishing House, 1972), 55.

[3] Ibid.

[4] Donald Gee, *The Pentecostal Movement*, rev. ed. (London: Elim, 1949; original ed. 1941), 5.

[5] Steve Durasoff, *Bright Wind of the Spirit* (Englewood Cliffs: Prentice-Hall, 1972), 51.

[6] See Vinson Synan, "The Rain Falls in America," in his *In the Latter Days. The Outpouring of the Holy Spirit in the Twentieth Century* (Ann Arbor: Servant Books, 1984), 43–54, esp. 44–45.

[7] Carl Brumback, *A Sound From Heaven* (1961; reprint, Springfield, Mo.: Gospel Publishing House, 1977), 92.

[8] Articles 7 and 9 (article 8 sets forth the "initial evidence" doctrine) of the AG *Statement of Fundamental Truths* are essentially an expanded version of what is compressed into article 7 of the Alliance *Statement of Faith* regarding the ministry of the Holy Spirit in the life of the believer. Compare

(2) the hymns of Simpson; (3) the books of Simpson, Pardington, Tozer, and others; (4) the terminology "Gospel Tabernacle," which, when supplemented with "Full," became a popular name for churches among Pentecostals; (5) the polity of the early Alliance society, after which the AG was styled; (6) a worldwide missionary vision; and (7) numerous leaders converted and trained in Alliance circles.[9]

Most recently, in her masterful analysis of the history of the AG, Edith Blumhofer spotlighted Simpson as one of those who "vigorously proclaimed in evangelical settings" elements of the Pentecostal message "long before the rise of Pentecostalism."[10] She drew attention specifically to Simpson's gospel of healing, premillennial eschatology, and his christocentric view of sanctification as providing an important prelude to Pentecostalism.[11] In many respects Blumhofer built on the thesis of Wesleyan scholar Donald Dayton, who had demonstrated that the basic "Fourfold pattern" of Pentecostal theology as it evolved in the early 1900s was clearly anticipated in the holiness and evangelical healing movements of the nineteenth century of which Simpson and the Alliance were a part.[12]

William W. Menzies, *Anointed to Serve. The Story of the Assemblies of God* (Springfield, Mo.: Gospel Publishing House, 1971), Appendix A, 388, and the *Manual of The Christian and Missionary Alliance* (Nyack, N.Y.: Christian and Missionary Alliance, 1978), 11–12. Admittedly, the AG's doctrine of sanctification is more of a hybrid reflecting both Wesleyan and Calvinistic motifs. On this subject see Dennis Leggett, "The Assemblies of God Statement on Sanctification," *Paraclete* 25 (Spring 1991): 19–27.

[9] John T. Nichol, *Pentecostalism*, rev. ed. (Plainfield, N.J.: Logos International, 1977), 55, identifies as one of the causes of the early success of Pentecostalism the fact that "scores of Pentecostal leaders had been nurtured in Simpson's Christian and Missionary Alliance Society."

[10] Edith L. Blumhofer, *The Assemblies of God* (Springfield, Mo.: Gospel Publishing House, 1989), vol. 1 (to 1941): 18.

[11] Ibid., 25–26, 29–31, 61–64.

[12] Dayton, *Theological Roots of Pentecostalism*, 21f., esp. 22, where he alludes to A. B. Simpson's "Four-fold Gospel" as a seminal expression of Pentecostal themes. The proliferation of holiness denominations toward the close of the nineteenth century and the spread of holiness spirituality beyond the Methodist tradition are discussed in Dieter, *The Holiness Revival of the Nineteenth Century*, 236–75; and George M. Marsden, *Fundamentalism and American Culture* (New York: Oxford University Press, 1980), 93–96.

Early Points of Contact Between Pentecostalism and the Alliance

The present trend among Pentecostal historians to cast Simpson in the role of a Pentecostal forerunner has its roots in the past perceptions of Pentecostal pioneers who had firsthand exposure to his movement. An examination of the sources reveals the appreciative attitude of several prominent early personalities toward the contribution made by Simpson and his colleagues to their spiritual journeys. In some cases, the eschatologically charged spirituality of the early Alliance fueled the expectation of first-generation Pentecostals that as a new century dawned, the full New Testament experience of Spirit baptism with accompanying supernatural manifestations would be restored to the modern church.

Charles Parham and Agnes Ozman

Charles A. Parham (1873–1929), Pentecostal patriarch and founder of the Apostolic Faith movement, had been successively a Congregationalist, Methodist, and holiness preacher prior to his Pentecostal experience in 1901. In late June 1900 he left his Bethel Healing Home in Topeka, Kansas, to visit various holiness and healing centers in the eastern United States. Included in his itinerary was Simpson's Missionary Training Institute recently relocated from New York City north on the Hudson River to Nyack.[13] Impressed by the national reputations of Simpson and his Baptist friend, Adoniram J. Gordon, Parham had frequently reprinted their writings in the *Apostolic Faith*, which was first published in 1899 and was coedited by him.[14]

In September 1900 Parham returned to Topeka spiritually dissatisfied. He expressed his conviction that the pinnacle of the apostolic gospel had not yet been attained:

---

[13] For documentation of this trip, see *Apostolic Faith* (Baxter Springs, Kan.) 2 (July 1926): 1; Sarah E. Parham, *The Life of Charles F. Parham, Founder of the Apostolic Faith Movement* (Joplin, Mo.: Tri-State Printing, 1930), 48; and James R. Goff, Jr.'s analysis of Parham's venture in *Fields White Unto Harvest: Charles F. Parham and the Missionary Origins of Pentecostalism* (Fayetteville, Ark.: University of Arkansas, 1988), 59–61.

[14] Goff, *Fields White Unto Harvest*, 45–46.

> I returned home fully convinced that while many had obtained
> real experience in sanctification and the anointing that abideth,
> there still remained a great outpouring of power for the Chris-
> tians who were to close this age.[15]

For all their "deep religious thought" and experience of "the power
of the Holy Ghost," Parham rejected the theology of Simpson and
other holiness and healing advocates who equated the "baptism
of the Holy Spirit" with "the witness of [one's] sanctification."[16]
What thousands "termed and supposed" to be the baptism of the
Spirit was for Parham "a mighty anointing that abideth," just as John
Wesley and others enjoyed. The "Pentecostal Baptism of the Holy
Spirit" he desired was purportedly "a different thing entirely."[17]

Parham criticized these centers of holiness and healing
spirituality on two counts. Not only did they fall short of "the
account in Acts"[18] in Parham's estimation, but they also spawned
an offensive sectarian spirit. He censured those "Bible Schools"
(presumably including Simpson's Nyack) "Zions," (and) "colo-
nies" he had toured because they adhered to the doctrines "of one
man," which caused them to "become narrow, selfish . . . self
advancing; until denouncing and un-Christianizing all others,
they [came] to believe they [were] the only people."[19]

Despite Parham's attempt to distance himself from the
promoters of nineteenth-century holiness and healing spirituality, other Pentecostal pioneers who personally witnessed
Parham's ministry testified to the lingering influence of Simpson
upon him. Howard Goss, a founding father of the AG, described
Parham's strategy in Topeka, Kansas, "a few years prior to the
Pentecostal outpouring" as an effort to gather "a good congregation around the truths of Divine Healing: Sanctification much as
Dr. Simpson had taught it."[20] Even during the second Pentecostal
revival in Galena, Kansas, in 1903, Goss recalled Parham as "[preach-
ing] a clean holy life of victory for all believers, and the second

---

[15]As quoted in Sarah E. Parham, *Charles F. Parham*, 48.

[16]Charles Parham, *The Sermons of Charles Parham*, ed. Donald Dayton (New York: Garland, 1985; original ed. 1902), 29.

[17]Ibid., 29, 32.

[18]Ibid., 30–31.

[19]Ibid., 53.

[20]As quoted in Ethel E. Goss, *The Winds of God: The Story of the Early
Pentecostal Days (1901–1914) in the Life of Howard A. Goss* (New York: Comet
Press, 1958), 18.

work of grace as taught by Rev. A. B. Simpson" in conjunction with a vigorous healing ministry.[21]

Agnes Ozman (1870–1937), the first of Parham's Bethel Bible College students in Topeka to receive the coveted apostolic baptism of the Holy Spirit accompanied by what she assumed to be xenolalia on January 1, 1901, named Simpson among her esteemed spiritual teachers. As an adolescent she had experienced Methodist "sanctification." In 1894 Ozman visited Moody Bible Institute for a few days and followed that with a longer period of study at Simpson's Missionary Training Institute in New York City. In her autobiography she reflected on the significance of this experience for her spiritual formation. While there, she evidently imbibed the two major thrusts of Simpson and the early Alliance—a life of deeper dependence on the Holy Spirit combined with a commitment to evangelism at home and overseas. She wrote with warmth regarding her sojourn in New York:

> Our teachers were A. B. Simpson, [F. W.] Farr, [A. E.] Funk, [Henry] Wilson and Stephen Merritt. The latter had learned much about the workings of the Holy Ghost, and our hearts were blessed as we were admonished to trust Him to use us. . . . I enjoyed going to the different missions. We went regularly to the 8th Street Mission and at times to the Water Street Hadly Mission, Florence Critegan Mission. . . . At the Christian Mission Alliance Bible School we were privileged to bid farewell to many dear hearts who laid their lives down, going to Africa, China, India and Jerusalem.[22]

After leaving New York City, Ozman engaged in missionary work in Kansas City and eventually became a student at Parham's Bethel Bible College in Topeka, Kansas, which opened in October 1900.[23] In retrospect, Ozman's exposure to the Alliance, although brief, was an important transitional phase of her journey into Pentecostalism.

Ambrose J. Tomlinson, Thomas B. Barratt, and Andrew H. Argue

Agnes Ozman's respect for the extensive pneumatological knowledge of Stephen Merritt, one of Simpson's earliest asso-

---

[21]Ibid., 15.

[22]Agnes N. O. La Berge, *What God Hath Wrought. Life and Work of Mrs. Agnes N. O. LaBerge Née Miss Agnes N. Ozman* (n.d.; reprint, New York: Garland, 1985), 23.

[23]Ibid., 27, 28.

ciates, was echoed in the spiritual quest of another Pentecostal pioneer, Ambrose J. Tomlinson (1865–1943). An itinerant preacher of Quaker lineage, Tomlinson was elected in 1914 as the first general overseer of the Church of God (Cleveland, Tennessee). Following his conversion in 1892, Tomlinson searched out locations where special visitations of the Holy Spirit were occurring. His goal was to find the true "Church of God" where the proclamation of the word was being confirmed by miracles, signs and wonders, and gifts of the Holy Spirit according to the pattern of Acts.[24]

Among other places, his travels took him to New York City, where he contacted Stephen Merritt.[25] Though Tomlinson's diary offers little detail concerning the actual substance of his encounter with Merritt, it is a reasonable assumption that the subject of the baptism of the Holy Spirit was Tomlinson's primary agenda. Merritt was well known both within and beyond Alliance circles for his specialized instruction on the person and work of the Holy Spirit. His identification with Simpson most likely stemmed from a shared concern to recover the lost truths of a deeper spiritual life and divine healing.[26] Merritt's own experience of being filled with the Holy Spirit had been made all the more famous by the involvement of Sammy Morris, the Kru boy who made the perilous voyage from Liberia to New York to inquire of Merritt about the Holy Spirit.[27] Such was the extent of Merritt's international reputation as an authority on the subject.[28]

The Norwegian Methodist Thomas B. Barratt (1862–1940), hailed as "the apostle of the Pentecostal Movement in Europe,"[29] readily acknowledges in his autobiography that "some articles in

---

[24]A. J. Tomlinson, *Diary of A. J. Tomlinson*, ed. Homer A. Tomlinson, 2 vols. (New York: Church of God, 1949), vol. 1: 1901 to 1923, 23, 24.

[25]Ibid., 24.

[26]Merritt was listed in the first annual report of Simpson's society (1888) as an officer and vice-chairman of the Board of Managers. His name appeared on the list of board members as late as 1900.

[27]See the account of Merritt's experience of being filled with the Spirit in David J. Fant, Jr., "Early Associates of A. B. Simpson," *The Southeastern District Report of the Christian and Missionary Alliance* (May 1977): 15. He regarded himself as living in the "age of the Holy Ghost." See Merritt, "Honoring the Holy Ghost," WWW 7 (October 1886): 198–99.

[28]See Merritt's introductory endorsement of Simpson's two-volume *The Holy Spirit or Power from on High*, vol. 1:7–8.

[29]See Nils Bloch-Hoell's discussion of Barratt's impact on Scandinavia in *The Pentecostal Movement. Its Origin, Development and Distinctive Character* (Oslo: Universitetsforlaget, 1964), 75–86.

Dr. A. B. Simpson's magazine were a great help."[30] A pivotal event in Barratt's journey into Pentecostalism occurred in 1906 while he was staying in the Alliance guest house in New York City. After attending a communion service in the Gospel Tabernacle, conducted by Simpson's Episcopalian colleague Henry Wilson, Barratt sought for the baptism of the Holy Spirit and was "seized by the Holy Power of God throughout [his] whole being, and it swept through [his] whole body as well."[31] Five weeks later, Barratt received what he called the "full Pentecostal experience" with the evidence of speaking in tongues.[32] In an article published in *Living Truths*, a periodical edited anonymously by Simpson, Barratt explained the gift of tongues, which he received on November 15, as the seal to his "baptism of fire" which he had experienced in the Alliance guest house on October 7.[33]

During the interval between the time of the "first mighty outpouring on [his] soul" and his full reception of the baptism of the Holy Spirit, Barratt exchanged letters with friends in Los Angeles. His interest at this time was directed toward the nature of the gift of tongues and its relationship to Spirit baptism. The holiness circles in which Barratt had been moving in New York seemed to offer no teaching on these subjects; he was thus motivated to communicate with the Azusa Street Mission and Charles Parham's Apostolic Faith movement.[34]

Barratt was exceedingly complimentary of Simpson. He both admired his ability to raise large sums of money for world missions and reckoned "him to be one of the greatest preachers of [his] day."[35]

On the Canadian scene, Andrew H. Argue (1868–1959), a realtor from Winnipeg who along with his family emerged as a

---

[30]Thomas B. Barratt, *The Work of T. B. Barratt* (1927; reprint, New York: Garland, 1985), 107–8. In his testimony, "How I Obtained My Pentecost," published in Simpson's magazine, Barratt esteemed Alliance teaching on consecration and the crisis of the deeper life and dialogue with some of Simpson's pastoral colleagues as steppingstones to his Pentecostal experience (CMAW 26 [November 3, 1906]: pagination obscured). Barratt's testimony was also later published in the *Pentecostal Evangel*: "After the Baptism of Fire in New York 1906," PE (May 9, 1925): 2–3.

[31]Barratt, *Work*, 111–14.

[32]Ibid., 124.

[33]T. B. Barratt, "The Seal of My Pentecost," LT 6 (December 1906): 735–38, esp. 736.

[34]Barratt, *Work*, 121–24.

[35]Ibid., 121.

potent evangelistic force in Canadian Pentecostalism, had contact with A. B. Simpson in 1906.[36] His encounter with Simpson in Winnipeg prepared him for his initiation into Pentecostalism. At a special healing service Simpson prayed for Argue's relief from a physical ailment. Argue's daughter later recalled the incident:

> [Simpson] prayed for father for healing from a chronic internal trouble. No immediate change was apparent. But just twenty-four hours later, like a flash of lightning the healing power of God went through him and the work was done.[37]

Argue's physical healing "greatly inspired faith in his heart" and intensified a process of spiritual awakening that climaxed in his reception of the baptism of the Holy Spirit with tongues in Chicago the following year.[38]

Alice Flower, Alice Garrigus, and Lilian Yeomans

Pentecostal women besides Agnes Ozman also testified to the formative influence of Simpson and the Alliance on their spiritual development. Alice Flower (b. 1890), wife of J. Roswell Flower, the first general secretary of the AG, remembered her mother and others forming a "little prayer circle" in Indianapolis that grew to be "the largest Christian and Missionary Alliance branch in the middle-west."[39] During her youth she claimed to have been profoundly impacted by the Alliance's Fourfold Gospel:

> I remember kneeling in the gallery of the old [Indianapolis] Gospel Tabernacle to make a deep consecration to God, calling it as was so common then, an experience of sanctification.[40]

---

[36]See Gloria G. Kulbeck, *What God Hath Wrought* (Toronto: Pentecostal Assemblies of Canada, 1958), 139–40, 142–43, 167, 176–77, for a more complete account of Argue's founding contribution to Canadian Pentecostalism; cf. Thomas Wm. Miller, "The Significance of A. H. Argue for Pentecostal Historiography," *Pneuma* 8 (Fall 1986): 120–58.

[37]Zelma Argue, *Contending for the Faith* (Winnipeg: Messenger of God, 1928), 17.

[38]Zelma Argue, *A Vision and a Vow. The Story of My Mother's Life* (Springfield, Mo.: Gospel Publishing House, n.d.), 37–38; cf. Kulbeck, *What God*, 139.

[39]Alice R. Flower, *Grace for Grace. Some Highlights of God's Grace in the Daily Life of the Flower Family* (Springfield, Mo.: privately published, 1961), 25.

[40]Ibid., 26; cf. Flower, *Seventy Years of Pentecostal Blessing* (privately published), 15–16, for her later reflections on her youthful quest to be

Especially memorable to Flower were the missionary conferences conducted there annually by Simpson. She credited them with "[doing] something to [her] as a child which [had] only intensified through the years."[41] Her recollection of Simpson's "searching missionary message" was that it was "delivered quietly but most impressively."[42]

It was in January 1907, "following the afternoon service in the [Indianapolis Alliance] Gospel Tabernacle" in "an after-meeting for testimony, praise and prayer," that she first heard a report about the outbreak of tongues speaking at the Azusa Street Mission in Los Angeles. Accompanied by her mother, an ardent seeker of Pentecostal experience, Flower attended a non-Alliance "tarrying meeting" on Easter Sunday the same year, a day when "the Day of Pentecost [came] in [her] life."[43] On his first visit to Indianapolis after Flower had received her Spirit baptism with tongues, Simpson affirmed her in her experience of the fullness of the Spirit and requested that she send him a written account of it. For Flower, this remained into her senior years as a "precious memory, for as a young girl [she] greatly revered this man of God."[44]

More indirectly, Alice Garrigus (1858–1949), a Congregationalist from Connecticut, also came under the influence of the Alliance in the course of her journey into Pentecostalism. She received the Pentecostal baptism with tongues at the conclusion of an Alliance camp meeting at Old Orchard Beach, Maine, in 1906. Having had no immediate contact with Simpson, Garrigus did associate temporarily with Minnie Draper, who had been both converted and healed in the Alliance. As one of Simpson's prominent female colleagues, Draper had assisted him in Alliance conventions held at Rocky Springs, Pennsylvania, New York City, and Old Orchard, Maine.[45] Garrigus went on to become the founding mother of the Pentecostal Assemblies of Newfoundland.

"wholly sanctified" as the preparation for her reception of the Pentecostal message of Spirit baptism with tongues in 1907.

[41]Flower, *Grace for Grace*, 27.

[42]Ibid., 26.

[43]See the chapter "My Day of Pentecost," in Flower, *Grace for Grace*, 31–36.

[44]Alice Reynolds Flower, "The Ministry of 'Brother Tom,' " in *Touched by the Fire*, ed. Wayne Warner (Plainfield, N.J.: Logos International, 1978), 33–34.

[45]Burton K. Janes, *The Lady Who Came. The Biography of Alice Belle Garrigus, Newfoundland's First Pentecostal Pioneer*, 1858–1908, 2 vols. (St. John's,

No one in early Pentecostal circles showed more deference to Simpson's practice and teaching of divine healing than the Canadian-born Lilian Yeomans (1861–1942). By vocation she was a physician and surgeon, having graduated from the University of Michigan's department of medicine. In later years she served as a Bible teacher on the faculty of the Lighthouse of International Foursquare Evangelism (L.I.F.E. Bible College) founded in Los Angeles by the Pentecostal healing evangelist Aimee Semple McPherson.[46]

In her book *Healing from Heaven* (1926), Yeomans identified numerous persons as part of the "revival of a faith for healing" that had been building gradually since the Protestant Reformation. She saw John Alexander Dowie (under whom she had been miraculously cured of narcotic addiction in 1898) and A. B. Simpson, however, as worthy of special honor in this historical crescendo of healing truth.[47] A chapter in her *Balm of Gilead* (1936) entitled "Himself" echoed Simpson's famous address by the same title, delivered at the London Bethshan Healing and Holiness Conference in 1885.[48] Another of Yeomans's publications, *The Royal Road to Health-Ville* (1938), bore the subtitle *Some Simple Talks About Divine Healing*, an evident adaptation of Simpson's earlier *Friday Meeting Talks* (1894).[49] On occasion, Yeomans went beyond an admiration for Simpson's life and healing ministry to the point of depending on his exegesis of pertinent biblical texts as well. In *Divine Healing Diamonds* (1933), she cited approvingly Simpson's

---

Nfld.: Good Tidings Press, 1982), 1:100–107; cf. Gary B. McGee's article on Draper in DPCM, 250. The schedule for the Old Orchard convention in August 1907 shows Draper as giving a "special testimony" on "The Spirit-filled Life" as well as participating in daily inquiry meetings for divine healing ("Programme of the Old Orchard Convention," CMAW 28 |August 3, 1907|: 56).

[46]On Yeomans's contact with Pentecostalism in 1907, see DPCM, 907.

[47]Lilian B. Yeomans, *Healing from Heaven* (Springfield, Mo.: Gospel Publishing House, 1926), 111–16. For an account of her healing in Simpson's magazine, see "Out of the Depths," CMAW 29 (February 15, 1908): 330–31, 338; cf. Lilian Yeomans, "Thirty-five Years of Divine Health," TF 53 (July 1933): 167–68.

[48]Lilian B. Yeomans, *Balm of Gilead* (Springfield, Mo.: Gospel Publishing House, 1935), 34–39, esp. 39.

[49]Lilian B. Yeomans, *The Royal Road to Health-Ville* (Springfield, Mo.: Gospel Publishing House, 1938).

comments on Luke 6:6–11.[50] She even showed an appreciation for Simpson's poetry.[51]

Aimee Semple McPherson and George Jeffreys

Aimee Semple McPherson (1890–1944), founder of the International Church of the Foursquare Gospel, and George Jeffreys (1889–1962), who established the Elim Foursquare Gospel Alliance, are examples of the indirect, though nonetheless real, influence of Simpson and the early Alliance on Pentecostalism. McPherson claimed that she received her "Foursquare Gospel" directly by divine revelation. The phrase had allegedly been given to her by the Holy Spirit during a sermon on "The Vision of Ezekiel" (based on Ezekiel 1:1–28), which she preached in an Oakland revival campaign in 1922, the year prior to the opening of her Angelus Temple in Los Angeles.[52]

Contrary to McPherson's own claims to originality, however, Foursquare historian James Bradley contended that McPherson in fact owed a large unacknowledged debt to Simpson.[53] The Foursquare Gospel—Christ as Savior, Baptizer in the Holy Spirit, Healer, and Coming King, though first publicly proclaimed by McPherson from the podium in Oakland in 1922, bore marked semblance to Simpson's "Fourfold Gospel," enunciated in his writings and popularized by Alliance preachers across the continent for three decades preceding McPherson's meteoric rise to stardom. Bradley has further shown McPherson's sermon "Lost and Restored," a de facto manifesto of the Foursquare movement, to be substantially borrowed from Simpson's *The Gospel of the Kingdom* (1890).[54] In the same vein, the official Foursquare logo,

---

[50]Lilian B. Yeomans, *Divine Healing Diamonds* (Springfield, Mo.: Gospel Publishing House, 1933), 16.

[51]See Lilian B. Yeomans, *Resurrection Rays* (Springfield, Mo.: Gospel Publishing House, 1930), 25, for an allusion to one of Simpson's poems.

[52]Aimee Semple McPherson, "The Foursquare Gospel in the Foursquare Way," *Bridal Call* 8 (August 1924): 18–20; cf. idem, *The Foursquare Gospel* (Los Angeles: Echo Park Evangelistic Association, 1946), ch. 2: "How the Foursquare Gospel Was Conceived," 19–24.

[53]James E. Bradley, "A. B. Simpson and the Origins of the Pentecostal Movement. Response to John M. Sawin's Paper" (Paper delivered at the Society for Pentecostal Studies, Costa Mesa, Calif., November 15, 1986).

[54]A. B. Simpson, *The Gospel of the Kingdom*.

consisting of a cross, a laver (representing healing), a dove, and a crown, varied only minimally from the Alliance's Fourfold emblem with its cross, laver (indicating the sanctifying grace of God), pitcher of oil, and crown. For Bradley, it was more than coincidence that the biblical rallying cry of the Foursquare denomination, Hebrews 13:8, was also the theme of the only Simpson hymn included in the Foursquare hymnal. When judged in its totality, the evidence seemed to point to "the real creative mind behind the Foursquare Church [as] not that of Aimee Semple McPherson, but that of Albert Benjamin Simpson."[55]

McPherson's packaging of the Pentecostal message in terminology that harked back to traditional Alliance themes invariably resonated with Alliance people who attended her revival meetings. R. H. Moon, a pastor from Oakland, California, gave the following favorable report of McPherson's ministry at a time when Alliance spiritual distinctives were beginning to wane:

> As a pastor who sat on the platform and listened to almost every one of [her] messages, I am glad to say that nothing but a Scriptural, sane, old-fashioned gospel was preached. There was not even a tinge of fanaticism or wild fire present in any of the meetings. . . .

> Personally, I was glad for the message of the necessity of the baptism with the Holy Ghost for the believers subsequent to conversion. It is this message that has precipitated a revival in my own church and has rekindled the old passion for souls.[56]

Mrs. Emma Whittemore, another of Simpson's distinguished early female associates, who gained international renown for her Door of Hope homes for prostitutes, commended the young Pentecostal evangelist as "very humble and childlike, and surely . . . filled with the Holy Ghost."[57] Through Simpson's ministry, Whittemore was healed of a serious spinal injury in 1884;[58] her testimony of a subsequent healing as well as of receiving the baptism of the Holy Spirit with tongues in 1919 at one of McPherson's conven-

---

[55]Bradley, "A. B. Simpson," 3–5.

[56]As quoted in Aimee Semple McPherson, This is That. Personal Experiences, Sermons and Writings of Aimee Semple McPherson, Evangelist (Los Angeles: Echo Park Evangelistic Association, 1926), 492.

[57]Mrs. E. M. Whittemore, "Healed and Filled with the Spirit," TF 39 (January 1919): 9.

[58]Mrs. E. M. Whittemore, "Conquered and Healed," Thy Healer 21 (November 1, 1884): 283–85.

tions in Philadelphia was printed in McPherson's magazine *The Bridal Call*. She joyfully recounted that:

> dear Mrs. McPherson saw me kneeling. . . . She came and said just a few words in prayer. I hadn't been there very long before I saw no man but Jesus only, and some way the power of the Holy Ghost came in, and in a wonderful, marvellous manner the Lord spoke to me as never before. Some words, I don't know what, issued forth from my lips. Sister McPherson interpreted them afterward as something about "the Bride is getting herself ready." A wealth of love was poured forth into my soul.[59]

Though the mature years of Simpson's and McPherson's ministries were not contemporary, the respective movements spawned by the two personalities did overlap chronologically, making it possible for persons to be dual Alliance/Foursquare spiritual beneficiaries. The eyewitness reports of Moon and Whittemore, two such persons, further substantiate Bradley's conclusion regarding the natural kinship between Simpson's Fourfold and McPherson's Foursquare gospels.[60] The affinity between these two traditions was seemingly symbolized later when Paul Rader, Simpson's presidential successor (who resigned in 1924), did a three-month substitution for McPherson at Angelus Temple in 1926.[61] The previous year Walter M. Turnbull, pastor of the Gospel Tabernacle in New York and foreign missionary secretary of the Alliance, had preached there from one of Simpson's favorite texts.[62]

---

[59]Mrs. Emma M. Whittemore, "Testimony," *Bridal Call* 2 (November 1918): 3.

[60]In this context, see the favorable evaluation of McPherson given by the Canadian Alliance preacher Oswald Smith, who visited Angelus Temple in 1925. Smith's article, "The World Beats a Path to Her Door," first appeared in his *Tabernacle News* (March 1925) and was reprinted in McPherson's *Bridal Call* 8 (May 1925): 22–23, 34. Of importance is Smith's doubt that McPherson believed in tongues as the initial evidence of the baptism of the Holy Spirit, though McPherson evidently leaned in that direction as shown in her "Foursquare Fundamentals," *Bridal Call* 12 (November 1928): 17.

[61]On the relationship between Rader and McPherson during the latter's troubled years, see Larry Eskridge, "Only Believe: Paul Rader and the Chicago Gospel Tabernacle, 1922–1933" (M.A. thesis, University of Maryland, 1985), 208–11.

[62]See McPherson's reprint of Turnbull's message delivered on June 21, 1925, "Bringing Back the King," *Bridal Call* 9 (September 1925): 10–12, 25–26.

Establishing a relationship between George Jeffreys, founder and leader of the Elim Foursquare Alliance in Britain, and the Christian and Missionary Alliance is admittedly tenuous. The similarities between the two movements, however, deserve comment.[63] In his book *Healing Rays* (1932), Jeffreys paid respect to Simpson as one who was "revered" because of "his faithful service in the Kingdom of God" and his leading of many into the truth of divine healing.[64] Jeffreys's adoption of "Foursquare" terminology is most likely traced to his ministry tour in Canada and the United States during 1924, when he encountered Aimee Semple McPherson's modified version of Simpson's Fourfold gospel. In a manner similar to McPherson, Jeffreys argued for the biblical indigenousness of the expression "Foursquare" without crediting any other historical source.[65]

The obvious parallels between Jeffreys's Elim movement and Simpson's Alliance, however, are hard to ignore. As in the case of the development of Simpson's organizations, Jeffreys's ecumenical vision, mirrored in the Elim Foursquare Gospel Alliance of the British Isles that he established in 1926, succumbed to a process of denominationalization in the twentieth century that led to the organization's name being changed to Elim Pentecostal Church.[66] Assessed doctrinally, Jeffreys and the Elim movement seemed more closely aligned at certain points with Simpson and the Alliance than with American Pentecostalism. Elim's rejection of speaking in tongues as the initial evidence of Spirit baptism and its affirmation of the continuation of gifts of

---

[63] My thinking was encouraged in this direction during a personal visit with Professor Walter Hollenweger at the University of Birmingham in June 1989.

[64] George Jeffreys, *Healing Rays* (London: Elim, Ltd., 1932), 133.

[65] George Jeffreys, *The Miraculous Foursquare Gospel—Doctrinal* (London: Elim, 1929), 1:1. Donald Gee's insistence that Jeffreys's meeting with McPherson at Angelus Temple in 1924 was not premeditated, and that despite the similarity in name the two organizations had "no official connection," borders on special pleading. Gee's desire to distance Jeffreys from McPherson stems more from his European reserve for "the city of Hollywood and the dramatic" than from any impartial historical analysis. See *Wind and Flame* (Croydon, England: Heath Press, 1967), 120. On McPherson's contact with Jeffreys in England in 1928, see Thompson Eade, "Britain Goes Foursquare," *Bridal Call* 12 (January 1929): 19, 30–31, esp. 31.

[66] See Walter J. Hollenweger, *The Pentecostals* (Peabody, Mass.: Hendrickson, reprint 1988), 200–201, for a summary of doctrinal differences between the Elim Churches and American Pentecostalism.

the Spirit within the context of a prescribed biblical order recalled Simpson's own convictions. Interestingly, T. J. McCrossan, a Presbyterian pastor-author with Alliance sympathies writing in the 1930s, distinguished Jeffreys's work in the British Isles from American Pentecostalism on the basis of the healing evangelist's refusal either to condone fanaticism or to endorse the doctrine of tongues as the initial evidence of Spirit baptism. In the light of Jeffreys's position on Spirit baptism and healing in the atonement, and his commitment to maintaining in his meetings a balanced blend of order and freedom in the expression of miraculous spiritual gifts under the sovereignty of the Holy Spirit, McCrossan viewed his doctrine and ministry as similar to that of Simpson and the Alliance.[67]

The Assemblies of God—A Case of Denominational Indebtedness

Of the new family of Pentecostal denominations that has its roots at Azusa Street, none is more indebted to Simpson and the early Alliance than the Assemblies of God (AG), which was officially formed in 1914 in Hot Springs, Arkansas, and subsequently emerged as the largest white Pentecostal denomination in the United States. During its fledgling years, the AG profited immensely from the important contributions made by a core of individuals who were spiritually mentored by Simpson and unwittingly groomed in his organization for skillful leadership roles in the AG after they exited the Alliance. AG historian Carl Brumback first enumerated them: J. W. Welch, Frank M. Boyd, D. W. Kerr, John Coxe, Herbert Cox, John Waggoner, David McDowell, E. F. M. Staudt, William I. Evans, A. G. Ward, George N. Eldridge, Louis and Josephine Turnbull, R. E. Sternall, C. A. McKinney, G. F. Bender, William W. Simpson, Noel Perkin, Alice Reynolds Flower, J. T. Boddy, Joseph Tunmore, and J. E. Kistler.[68]

---

[67]See T. J. McCrossan, *Christ's Paralyzed Church X-rayed* (Youngstown, Ohio: published by Rev. C. E. Humbard, 1937), 223–24, 233–36, 267–68, 312–13, 340–41.

[68]See Brumback, *Sound*, 92. He wrongly identified D. W. Myland, Minnie Draper, William Cramer, and Frederick Reel as holding AG credentials. For a less complete list, see Robert Mapes Anderson, *Vision of the Disinherited* (New York: Oxford University Press, 1979), 145.

An analysis of the AG's early organizational, theological, and spiritual development yields abundant evidence as to the influence exerted by a nucleus of experienced former Alliance workers. These men and women provided the AG with part of its first-generation leadership. Their spiritual maturity and discernment, creative energy, organizational ability, and literary skills constituted a resource utilized repeatedly in the consolidation of political and educational structures, the nurturing of spiritual life, the definition of mission, and the defense against heresy.

In the first four General Councils of the AG, former Alliance members were at the forefront of proceedings. The first Executive Presbytery created and elected at Hot Springs, Arkansas (1914), consisted of twelve representatives including Daniel W. Kerr of Cleveland, Ohio, and John W. Welch of Baxter Springs, Kansas.[69] At the second General Council, held in Chicago (1914), when the Executive Presbytery was expanded from twelve to sixteen persons to "make it more representative," David H. McDowell of Tottenville, New York, was added.[70] The third council in St. Louis (1915) witnessed a further rise in the public profile of individuals with an Alliance past. Welch was elected as temporary chairman. The preceding chairman and his assistant chairman failed to appear at the opening session in St. Louis since they had both defected to the Oneness movement.[71] Welch went on to hold the position as general chairman of the AG from 1915 to 1919 and again from 1923 to 1925.[72] In addition to his duties as chairman, he was also commissioned by the St. Louis council as the missionary secretary-treasurer, responsible for "the receiving and disbursing of all missionary contributions."[73] At the fourth council in St. Louis (1916), out of a need to accommodate the rapid

---

[69]*Combined Minutes of the General Council of the Assemblies of God in the United States of America, Canada and Foreign Lands held at Hot Springs, Ark. Apr. 2–12, 1914 and at the Stone Church, Chicago, Ill. Nov. 15–29, 1914*, 9; cf. Irvine J. Harrison, "A History of the Assemblies of God" (Th.D. diss., Berkeley Baptist Divinity School, 1954), 107.

[70]Harrison, "History," 109–10.

[71]Ibid., 111, 143.

[72]Ibid., 111–12; cf. *Fiftieth Anniversary of the Assemblies of God* (n.p., n.d.), 11, 12.

[73]Harrison, "History," 115. On the largeness of Welch's spiritual stature in the early AG, see the posthumous tributes paid to him by J. Roswell Flower, Noel Perkin, Fred Vogler, and Stanley Frodsham in PE (July 29, 1939): 1–5.

expansion of the movement, two groups of Presbyters were created. Welch and Kerr continued to serve on the five-member Executive Presbytery. Of the eleven members constituting the newly formed General Presbytery, three had Alliance background: David McDowell, J. T. Boddy, and George N. Eldridge.[74] Moreover, the minutes of the fourth council record that D. W. Kerr delivered the introductory Sunday morning message and then toward the close of the council took the floor again by special request to preach on the deity of Christ, a sermon received "with great profit to all."[75] Ironically, it was two "Alliance" men, Kerr and Eldridge, who inspired the formation of the Southern California District Council of the AG in 1919. The Southern California district council had headquarters in Los Angeles, close to the original fount of Pentecostalism.[76] Eldridge and his son-in-law, Louis Turnbull, a former Alliance missionary to India, served as the district's first two chairmen.

Early Pentecostal educational institutions bore the stamp of those with an Alliance heritage. For example, Bethel Bible Training School, an independent effort born in Bethel Pentecostal Assembly in Newark, New Jersey, in 1916, had as its first principal W. W. Simpson, who had served as an Alliance missionary in China and Tibet. He was succeeded by Frank Boyd (1917–23) and William Evans (1923–29), both of whom had graduated from Simpson's Missionary Training Institute in 1910 and 1911 respectively.[77]

The establishment of the AG school Central Bible Institute (CBI) in Springfield, Missouri, in 1922 was the fruit of an initiative on the part of the General Council to legitimize education in an immature movement that feared formalism and lacked appreciation for the strengths of an institutionally trained leadership. At a point in the history of the AG when the value of personal, suprarational religious experience was extolled over

---

[74]Harrison, "History," 123; cf. *Combined Minutes of the General Council of the Assemblies of God, 1914–1917* (Springfield, Mo.: Gospel Publishing House, n.d.), 4.

[75]*Minutes of the General Council of the Assemblies of God in the United States of America, Canada and Foreign Lands held at Bethel Chapel, St. Louis, Mo., Oct. 1–7, 1916*, 3, 9.

[76]See the typed "Notice of the Formation of the Southern California District Council of The Assemblies of God," in the AG Archives, Springfield, Mo.

[77]*Memoirs of Bethel 1916–1929* (published privately by Paul and Dorothy Emery, n.d.), 3.

that of higher education, the triumvirate of Kerr, Boyd, and eventually Evans labored relentlessly on behalf of the cause of Christian education. Evans, a former president of the Student Missionary Band at Nyack, served as dean of CBI for twenty-six years (1929–54).[78] Throughout his lengthy tenure as dean, Evans was recognized as an "awesome presence," who contributed much to the school's spiritual credibility.[79] Kerr and Boyd punctuated issues of the *Pentecostal Evangel* with articles aimed at updating the constituency on the progress of the Institute, defending the necessity of Bible schools, and persuading readers to support financially the new educational venture.[80] Their labors were augmented by those of David McDowell, who rose in the ranks to assistant chairman of the General Council.[81]

In language somewhat reminiscent of Simpson's Missionary Training Institute's idyllic setting at Nyack, Kerr advertised the future campus of CBI as a

> tract of land . . . just a little outside of the City limits in a quiet, oak-timbered spot, just the place for worship, rest and study. A good sized stream of clear spring water flows near by, part of which will be available for any purpose for which the Institute may wish to use it.[82]

---

[78]Ibid., 5.

[79]Blumhofer, *Assemblies*, 1:323; cf. W. I. Evans's articulation of and commitment to the Pentecostal vision in "This River Must Flow," PE (August 3, 1946): 2–3.

[80]See D. W. Kerr: "Bible Schools are Necessary," PE (April 15, 1922): 5; "The Purpose of Bible Schools," PE (May 27, 1922): 4; "The Central Bible School of the Assemblies of God," PE (August 5, 1922): 4; "Opening of the Central Bible Institute," PE (September 30, 1922): 4; "The New Addition to the Pentecostal Evangel Family," PE (October 14, 1922): 4; "Central Bible Institute News," PE (November 11, 1922): 7; " 'Yours' or 'Ours,' Which?" PE (November 25, 1922): 4; "Central Bible Institute. Some More News," PE (December 9, 1922): 4; "Prospective Students," PE (December 23, 1922): 9; "A Forward Look," PE (March 3, 1923): 11; Frank Boyd: "An Eye-opener or Enlarged Vision," PE (April 21, 1923): 4–5; "The Central Bible Institute. Concerning September 2," PE (September 1, 1923): 4; "Progress in the Building of Central Bible Institute. How Shall We Complete It?" PE (October 23, 1923): 8–9; "Christian Education in Relation to the Worldwide Missionary Program," PE (August 9, 1924): 7–8.

[81]David H. McDowell: "The Bible School," PE (December 1, 1923): 4–5; "The Central Bible Institute and the Financial Plan. Donations Dollars Dimes," PE (May 17, 1924): 5–6.

[82]D. W. Kerr, "The Central Bible Institute of the Assemblies of God," PE (August 19, 1922): 4. Early catalogues of Simpson's Missionary

As founding father of the school, Kerr considered his establishment of CBI in close proximity to denominational headquarters a crowning achievement in his life. Like a "Simeon of old,"
having witnessed the establishment of a Bible school in Springfield,
Kerr was prepared to "depart in peace," which he did in 1927.[83]

The younger Boyd's educational exploits were similarly
impressive. He was appointed principal of CBI in 1923. Later he
went on to advance the cause of education in the AG by serving
in numerous other capacities.[84] Most likely inspired by the model
of Simpson's Correspondence Bible School, Boyd's Berean structure targeted laypeople and ministers unable to attend one of the
AG's regional Bible institutes.[85] Complementing his educational
innovations, Boyd made a generous contribution to the corpus of
literature used in the training of a generation of pastors and
missionaries.[86]

Since so many graduates of Nyack transferred their loyalties from the Alliance to the AG, the three-year Bible institute
model perfected by A. B. Simpson and D. L. Moody, in which the
quasi-monastic atmosphere of the school was geared more to
spiritual development than to academics, became the official
strategy for the preparation of leadership. The transmission of
Simpson's educational vision through the medium of his former
colleagues and students has been fittingly preserved in the nam-

---

Training Institute at Nyack extolled the natural beauty of the campus and
stressed its conduciveness to study and spiritual refreshment. On the
influence of the Missionary Training Institute and Bethel Bible Training
School on the programmatic development of CBI, see Gary B. McGee, "For
the Training of . . . Missionaries," *Central Bible College Bulletin* (February
1984): 4–5.

[83]Joseph L. Vitello, "A History and Evaluation of the Attitudes of
the Assemblies of God Toward Post-Secondary Education" (M.A. thesis,
Central Bible Institute, n.d.), 10. On Kerr's pioneer involvement in AG
education at Springfield and elsewhere, see Blumhofer, *Assemblies*, 1:317–19.

[84]See Edith Waldvogel Blumhofer, *The Assemblies of God: A Popular
History* (Springfield, Mo.: Gospel Publishing House, 1985), 69; cf. B. M.
Stout, "Boyd, Frank Matthews" (1883–1984), DPCM, 94–95.

[85]Stout, "Boyd, Frank Matthews," 94–95. As an example of materials used, see Frank M. Boyd, *Correspondence School of the General Council of the
Assemblies of God. Prophetic Light* (Springfield, Mo.: Gospel Publishing House,
1948), Book I.

[86]See Frank M. Boyd: *Introduction to Prophecy* (Springfield, Mo.:
Gospel Publishing House, 1948); *God's Wonderful Book. The Origin, Lineage and
Influence of the Bible* (Springfield, Mo.: Gospel Publishing House, 1933); and
Ages and Dispensations (Springfield, Mo.: Gospel Publishing House, n.d.).

ing of five main buildings on the campus of Central Bible College (Institute until 1965) in Springfield after pioneers whose spiritual roots were in the Alliance.[87]

The organizational and educational contributions made by those who had come out of the Alliance were enhanced by their attempts to inculcate early AG doctrine and spirituality with a solidly christocentric focus in the tradition of Simpson's Fourfold Gospel. Their experience of the baptism of the Holy Spirit with tongues did not displace the "Jesus only" emphasis imbibed during their years in the Alliance. In 1924, a decade after the inception of the AG, David McDowell observed among the movement's constituents an unhealthy tendency to be absorbed in personal religious experience at the expense of the centrality of Christ. As a remedy against indulgent subjectivism, McDowell called for a return to authentic sanctification as understood in the traditional Alliance doctrine of the "indwelling Christ," which he maintained was "the vital point of Christianity."[88] His criticism of those in the movement enamored with "a religion of personal individual blessings" contained strains of Simpson's keynote hymn, "Himself" (1891), which elevated the Christ-life above the domain of blessings, feelings, and spiritual gifts. McDowell further beckoned fellow Pentecostals not to view the second coming of Christ as simply one element in a supernatural divine economy, alongside regeneration, Spirit baptism, latter rain, and miracles. Rather he urged them to see it as "THE program" to which all else was subordinate.[89]

That the third "fold" of Simpson's Fourfold Gospel—Christ as healer—also formed part of the early AG's spiritual milieu is at least partially due to the influence of those who both had been personally healed and had taught the doctrine of healing in the atonement during their years in the Alliance. For example, addressing the General Council in 1923, Daniel W. Kerr recounted his experience of divine healing while with the Alliance and invited all those present to receive Christ as their "family physi-

---

[87]See Gary B. McGee, "Pentecostal Awakenings at Nyack," *Paraclete* 18 (Summer 1984): 27. The particular Alliance individuals remembered are Eleanor Bowie, Frank M. Boyd, William I. Evans, J. Roswell Flower, and John W. Welch.

[88]David H. McDowell, "The Preeminent Christ," PE (December 6, 1924): 4.

[89]David H. McDowell, "The Purpose of the Coming of the Lord," PE (May 2, 1925): 2.

cian."[90] Tellingly, he concluded the chapter on healing in his *Waters in the Desert* with verses from Simpson's hymn "Healing in His Wings" (1897).[91]

In her discussion of the nineteenth-century wellsprings of Pentecostalism, AG historian Edith Blumhofer credits Simpson with having a wide impact on Pentecostals through his healing message. His focus on "Jesus Christ the same yesterday, and today, and for ever" (Hebrews 13:8), popularized in his hymnody, made Simpson one of those responsible for the bond between healing and the gospel so deeply embedded in the consciousness of American Pentecostalism.[92] The degree to which the early AG perpetuated the Alliance's theological stance on healing in the atonement is indicated by Article 12 of its Statement of Fundamental Truths, which dates to 1916 (drafted largely by Kerr). It reads: "Deliverance from sickness is provided for in the atonement, and is the privilege of all believers" (Isaiah 53:4, 5; Matthew 8:16, 17; James 5:14–16).[93] The definite influence of Simpson's gospel of healing, effectively mediated through his disciples, continued beyond their lifetime. More recently, an undated leaflet entitled *How to Receive and Keep Divine Healing*, disseminated by the denominational publishing house, consists entirely of a plagiarized digest of Simpson's tracts.[94] Throughout the twentieth century, AG authors have continued to draw attention to Simpson's importance in the healing revival of the nineteenth century while appealing to his teachings as precedent for the doctrines of divine healing to which they adhere.[95]

Former Alliance personalities, as heirs of Simpson's passion to proclaim the Fourfold Gospel around the world, were

[90]D. W. Kerr, "Our Family Physician," PE (October 20, 1923): 4.

[91]D. W. Kerr, *Waters in the Desert* (Springfield, Mo.: Gospel Publishing House, 1925), 103.

[92]Blumhofer, *Assemblies*, 1:29–31, esp. 31.

[93]The full text of the *Statement* is given in Menzies, *Anointed*, 384–90.

[94]*How to Receive and Keep Divine Healing* (Springfield, Mo.: Gospel Publishing House, n.d.), Tract No. 34–4536; compare Simpson's tracts *How to Retain Divine Healing* and *How to Receive and Retain Divine Healing* (New York: The Christian and Missionary Alliance, n.d.).

[95]See Carl Henry, *Christ the Great Physician* (Oakland, Calif.: privately published, 1946), 87–88; L. Thomas Holdcroft, *Divine Healing: A Comparative Study* (Springfield, Mo.: Gospel Publishing House, 1967), 25; Jesse K. Moon, *Divine Healing and the Problem of Suffering* (Waxahachie: Tex.: privately published, 1976), 61–62; Hugh Jeter, *By His Stripes* (Springfield, Mo.: Gospel Publishing House, 1977), 62.

leading figures in the cultivation of early AG foreign missionary awareness. In his promotion of international missions at a select gathering of AG leaders in 1924, David McDowell called those present to consider Simpson's vision of "a special Advent baptism," received toward the end of his ministry, as an incentive to "prepare young people" to engage in world evangelization.[96] Daniel Kerr's attempts to induce the AG to embrace a thoroughly missions-minded agenda were indefatigable. At the General Council in 1919, he spoke passionately on behalf of world missions:

> The law of missions had a beginning. Missions trickled down on the day of Pentecost. The Holy Spirit is missionary, Jesus Christ is missionary, the Father is missionary. Jesus Christ, when He had finished His missionary trip, sent the other Missionary down, and He is within us.[97]

Kerr further insisted that "the calling of the General Council and of the whole Pentecostal movement is distinctly missionary."[98] His commitment to the priority of missions gained him the reputation of being a "missionary crank."[99] Not only did Kerr propagate it at the theoretical level through speaking and writing, but his many years of Alliance-acquired expertise were put to good use in the implementation of structures for executing a missionary vision. The adoption by the early AG of successful Alliance tactics for promoting and supporting missions, such as pledge cards,[100] missionary prayer calendars,[101] and missionary conventions,[102] can be traced to Kerr's influence. He was respected by

---

[96]"Four Days with the Presbyters," PE (June 7, 1924); 5.

[97]"Some Good Things Said at the General Council Meeting," PE (November 1, 1919): 3.

[98]"Echoes of the Council," PE (November 1, 1919): 4.

[99]D. W. Kerr, "The Evangelization of the World," PE (October 17, 1925): 4; cf. idem, "The Missionary Outlook," PE (May 19, 1923): 2–3. Simpson's concern about the "neglected parts" of the world was reflected in Kerr's appeal for Pentecostals to evangelize the "neglected parts of the United States and Canada." See his general letter of December 19, 1919, addressed to "Co-laborers in the Master's Harvest-field," in the AG Archives, Springfield, Mo., and the posthumous statement in "Tributes to Brother Kerr," PE (April 16, 1927): 4: "He had a great missionary heart and has probably done more for our Pentecostal missionaries than any other man in the movement."

[100] "The 1918 General Council," CE (October 5, 1918): 3; "More About the Tenth General Council," PE (October 13, 1923): 3.

[101] "Missionary Prayer Calendar," CE (June 28, 1919): 4.

[102]"D. W. Kerr Has Offered His Services," PE (March 17, 1923): 12.

his colleagues as an "experienced hand" who was said to be "at his best in a Missionary Convention."[103] The combination of his Alliance-inherited commitment to missions and his unique ability to give legs to his vision resulted in his "enthusiastic" appointment as Missionary Field Secretary.[104]

Individuals who had acquired their missionary consciousness in Simpson's Alliance were not only instrumental in the AG's initial efforts to nurture a missionary vision and develop a strategy of its own, but as AG historian Gary McGee's careful research has confirmed, they also supplied the AG with a sizeable number of its first-generation missionaries. During the 1920s Nyack alumni constituted the largest representation of any one school serving in the AG missionary force.[105] Noel Perkin, who testified to having received his spiritual foundation in the Alliance, served as the AG foreign mission director from 1927 to 1959. In short, Perkin's policy was to some extent the translating of Alliance missiological principles into an AG context, with some modifications.[106]

Simpson's protégés who joined the AG not only inspired and gave direction to its overseas expansion but also played a key role in helping to prevent the young movement's near dissolution through theological controversy. They gave a guiding hand to its doctrinal development at a time when it was being internally destabilized by the Oneness movement, which arose out of the Worldwide Apostolic Faith Camp Meeting that began on April 15, 1913, near Pasadena, California. When novel "revelations" about the Godhead threatened to erode the orthodox trinitarian dogmatic base, Welch, Kerr, and J. Roswell Flower provided the front line of defense against the protagonists of a revived version of ancient modalism.[107] Welch chaired the critical General Council of 1915 and spearheaded the opposition against Oneness advocates, who initially made considerable gains at the expense of trinitarians.[108] Kerr and Flower discerned and tackled the doc-

---

[103] "Springfield's Good Convention," PE (June 2, 1923): 4; cf. Kerr's leadership in the AG-inspired, nondenominational Pentecostal Missionary Conferences in Gary B. McGee, "Missionary Conference, The," DPCM, 610.

[104] "D. W. Kerr Has Offered His Services," PE (March 17, 1923): 12.

[105] Gary B. McGee, *This Gospel Shall Be Preached*, 2 vols. (Springfield, Mo.: Gospel Publishing House, 1986, 1989), 1:62–63.

[106] Ibid., 1:129–43.

[107] The Oneness controversy is analyzed in detail in Blumhofer, *Assemblies*, 1:221–39.

[108] Joseph H. Howell, "The People of the Name: Oneness Pen-

trinal issues at stake in the controversy. Demonstrating his theological acumen, Kerr, as a member of the committee at the 1916
General Council whose mandate was to compose a doctrinal
statement, prepared a lengthy trinitarian apology, much of which
was incorporated into the Statement of Fundamental Truths.[109]
The Statement, clearly preoccupied with the Oneness issue, was
officially adopted by the Council.[110] Flower used his position as
office editor of the *Evangel*, the AG's official publication, to considerable advantage. He both strengthened "trinitarian" hold of
the periodical (its editor-in-chief, E. N. Bell, temporarily went
with the Oneness people) and strove to achieve a trinitarian
consensus among those swayed by the new teaching.[111] The irony
is that men indebted to Simpson and the Alliance for their spiritual formation found themselves fighting against a movement
that derived some of its popularity from the widespread acceptance of the Jesus-centered piety heralded in sermons and books
by Simpson and other Victorian evangelicals.[112]

The evidence for the formative influence of Simpson and
the Alliance on the early AG is most succinctly presented in the
case of the AG's official organ, the *Pentecostal Evangel* (previously
the *Weekly Evangel* and the *Christian Evangel*). In 1919 J. T. Boddy, a
member of the Alliance who had received his Spirit baptism with
tongues in 1907, was appointed editor.[113] In the same year (also
the year of Simpson's death) Simpson's classic *The Christ Life* was
advertised in the magazine as a "brief . . . simple . . . wonderfully
lucid and helpful" book that distinguished "nominal Christians"
from "real 'Jesus people.' "[114] The recommendation of other books
written by Simpson and his Nyack faculty continued in subsequent issues.[115] Respect for Simpson as part of the AG's spiritual

---

tecostalism in the United States" (Ph.D. diss., Florida State University,
1985), 41.

[109] Ibid., 44; cf. Blumhofer, *Assemblies*, 1:236.

[110] Howell, "People of the Name," 45.

[111] On Flower's role in the controversy see Blumhofer, *Assemblies*,
1:228–235.

[112] This observation has been made by David Arthur Reed, "Origins and Development of the Theology of Oneness Pentecostalism in the
United States," *Pneuma* 1 (Spring 1979): 32–33.

[113] See Stanley H. Frodsham, *With Signs Following*, rev. ed. (Springfield, Mo.: Gospel Publishing House, 1946), 45.

[114] Advertisement, PE (November 1919): 28.

[115] For example, see PE (November 11, 1922): 23, 24; PE (July 9,
1921): 13; PE (April 26, 1924): 16.

heritage did not diminish with the passage of time. The *Evangel* indices for 1950–64 show that no less than thirty-five excerpts from his writings appeared during the period, mostly on the subject of healing and holiness. Long after a generation of AG leaders who had Alliance backgrounds had passed from the scene, an appreciation for Simpson's legacy lived on.

SIMPSON AS PENTECOSTAL FORERUNNER

SOME HISTORIANS MIGHT BE duly suspicious of the concept of "forerunner" in that it could be perceived as an invention of a movement seeking to defend itself against accusations of heresy and innovation made by older, "orthodox," religious traditions. From this perspective, the use of the term would constitute a departure from the canons of historical objectivity. The purpose of this chapter, however, is not to portray A. B. Simpson as a proto-Pentecostal per se. Rather, the concept of Simpson as Pentecostal forerunner interprets him as one who was in dialogue (sometimes hostile) with the established churches of his time, in the context of which he raised questions and offered answers that anticipated some of the salient emphases of modern Pentecostalism. Without downplaying Simpson's criticisms of the Pentecostal movement (discussed in the next chapter), an in-depth analysis of his theology reveals several themes that surface as points of ideological continuity between himself and early Pentecostals. Of special interest in this regard are Simpson's restorationist and premillennial ideology, his doctrine of the baptism of the Holy Spirit, his understanding of spiritual gifts in the life of the church, and his hermeneutical approach to the book of Acts.

Simpson's Restorationist and Premillennial Ideology

Simpson's commitment to recovering the allegedly lost message and vitality of the New Testament church was an impulse generated by an age in which many nineteenth-century American evangelicals saw themselves as standing near the end of two millennia of church history, the conclusion of which was announced by a return to the pristine apostolic beginnings of Christianity. They rejected the prevalent cultural image of the later nineteenth century as a golden age of progress, even though it was concretized in the minds of the masses of western Europe and America by a proliferation of inventions that increased economic production, bettered the general standard of living, improved public communication, and made transportation cheaper and more efficient. Instead, these evangelical reformers promoted a quasi-utopian vision of primitive Christianity that served as a blueprint for the renewal and purification of the present church with all its ills. Such an idyllic portrait of Christian roots was animated by chiliastic expectations that God would soon directly intervene in world history and bring it to its long-awaited consummation—the establishment of the reign of Christ upon the earth. Premillennial eschatology, with its innate pessimism about the deteriorating condition of the world, contributed directly to the intensification of restorationist yearnings.[1]

Two of Simpson's turn-of-the-century publications were vintage expressions of his saturation in a *restorationist and premillennial* ideology. In a series of sermons given at a Gospel Tabernacle convention, published in 1897 under the title *The Present Truth*, he deplored the "progress of [the] times" as a devilish plot designed "to get the supernatural out of the Bible, out of the church ... out of ... individual Christian lives, and to reduce religion to a human science, obliterating everything that cannot be explained on a rational principle and from natural causes."[2] While society at

---

[1] On the upsurge in premillennialist fervor in American evangelicalism during the second half of the nineteenth century, see Weber, *Second Coming*, 43–64. Concerning the earlier outbreak of apocalyptic millenarianism at the beginning of the century, see Ernest Sandeen, "Millennialism," in *The Rise of Adventism*, ed. Edwin S. Gaustad (New York: Harper and Row, 1974), 104–18.

[2] A. B. Simpson, *The Present Truth* (South Nyack, N.Y.: Christian Alliance, 1897), 7–8.

large was "sinking to the low plane of naturalism and rationalism," Simpson called for the restoration of a supernaturally empowered church, which in the tradition of its first-century ancestor would be authenticated by "signs and wonders and . . . divers miracles and gifts of the Holy Spirit. . . . "[3] Such a "supernatural church," which Simpson envisioned as overriding historic denominational divisions derived from disputes over secondary doctrines, polity, and methods of ministry, could then accomplish the evangelization of the world, thereby setting the stage for Christ's coming.[4] For Simpson, a revival of the supernatural essence of Christianity was the only means of delivering the church of his time from an apostate condition brought on by succumbing to values of the age, hailed by many as socially progressive. Simpson sounded a note of apocalyptic alarm about the perils of modernism:

> Alas! Even in our democratic age the bribe of the world's favour and the popular applause of the multitude has [sic] proved as fatal to the church's purity and left her with Laodicea, which means to "please the people," basking in the smiles of the world, but standing on the very verge of the awful and impending judgment of her indignant and insulted Lord.[5]

In The Old Faith and the New Gospels (1911), first given in the form of addresses at Old Orchard, Maine, on the subject of Christianity and modernity, Simpson assailed the evils of the modern era, namely, Darwinian evolution, the higher criticism of the Bible, theological liberalism, philosophical moralism, *healing and spiritualist* cults, and socialism. He charged these movements collectively with inducing the political and moral destabilization of society, likening them to a "flotsam and jetsam on [a] great flood . . . sweeping away the landmarks of the past."[6] Worst of all, these "seething tides" of change were eroding "the great foundations of religious truth" and striking at the "Rock of Ages itself."[7] For Simpson, the intensity of the conflict between new and traditional values at the outset of the twentieth century intimated that the battle of "Armageddon" was "not far away."[8]

---

[3] Ibid., 105–6.

[4] Ibid., 64, 66–68, 79–80, 143–44.

[5] Ibid., 72.

[6] Simpson, The Old Faith and the New Gospels (New York: Alliance Press, 1911), 143.

[7] Ibid.

[8] Ibid., 8.

He concluded the book with a vigorous defense of premillennial eschatology despite its doom and gloom scenario of the end times. Contrary to the more fashionable postmillennial outlook, Simpson protested that premillennialism was nonetheless an equally viable interpretation of social reality:

> [Postmillenialism] is the dream and the constant watchword of the . . . church today. That is the brilliant optimism of many religious leaders and the great body of modern Social Reformers. We cannot deny to these men and women the merit of great sincerity and genuine enthusiasm. They hail the advent of modern progress, the forces of electricity, steam, radio, the wireless telegraph, the automobile, the airplane, the printing press, the university, the popular library, the progress of our time as the very beginning of the Golden Age. And if we for a moment point our fingers to the awful conditions that still exist, the poverty, the crime, the cruelty, the luxury, the licentiousness, the lust, the oppression, the Sabbath-breaking, the drunkenness, the increase of disorder and crime, they call us pessimists and charge us with holding back the wheels of the chariot of the Lord by the dead weight of our narrowness and conservatism.[9]

Not to be silenced by the social pundits of his age, Simpson dismissed postmillennialism as the delusion of "a nominal Christianity, lukewarm, Christless and ripe for judgment."[10]

Simpson's vision of a restored end-time church, fully endued with supernatural power and expectant of a personal advent of Christ bursting in upon an "astonished world"[11] to establish his millennial kingdom, was also fanned by his Zionist sympathies. The return of Jews to Palestine and the imminent prospect of the reestablishment of a Jewish state served as a timekeeper for Simpson's restorationist agenda.

In his *Gospel of the Kingdom* (1890) Simpson singled out the return of Jews to Palestine as one of the unmistakable signs of the end times. He noted the beginnings of the restoration of the Jewish people that had occurred with their emancipation in various European countries throughout the eighteenth and nineteenth centuries.[12] Simpson further lauded Zionism as the crystallization

---

[9] Ibid., 134.
[10] Ibid., 135.
[11] Ibid., 136.
[12] Simpson, The Gospel of the Kingdom, 178f.

of Hebrew patriotism, "destined to become a spontaneous and universal Jewish renaissance."[13] He noted that it had been exactly 1260 years from the Muslim conquest of Jerusalem in A.D. 636 to the birth of Zionism in 1896, thus fulfilling Daniel's prophecy.[14]

As part of the itinerary of a trip made in 1893 to investigate the state of Christian missions in the Middle East and the Orient, Simpson visited Palestine. With his observation of the progress of Jewish settlement in the region alongside the "naturally indolent, apathetic and indifferent" native Arab population, Simpson included an exhortation to Christians to pray for:

> the breaking of the Turkish yoke, the influx of a new population, and the preparation of the way for the return of the best classes of the Jewish people, the true "Kings of the East."[15]

So intense were Simpson's pro-Zionist sentiments that on the occasion of British General Allenby's capture of Jerusalem in 1918, he suffered a paralyzing stroke. His granddaughter concluded that "the rapture of [Allenby's entrance into Jerusalem] coupled with fifty years of a supernaturally active life was such a terrific shock to [Simpson's] whole system that he never recovered."[16] Zionist ideology—secular as it was—when sanctified by premillennial interpretations of biblical prophecies proved a fitting ally of Simpson's restorationist ecclesiology. In the apt words of one of Simpson's Canadian co-workers, Zionism was "a new shadow upon the Divine sundial."[17]

Interpreting church history within a restorationist framework, Simpson believed that the most significant feature of church history from the Protestant Reformation to his own time was the recovery of truths at the heart of the first-century apostolic gospel but obscured and forgotten in subsequent centuries. Speaking at

---

[13]Simpson, "Israel in the Light of Prophecy and Providence," LT 4 (August 1904): 439.

[14]Ibid.; cf. Daniel 12:7.

[15]Simpson, Larger Outlooks, 99.

[16]Katherine A. Brennen, Mrs. A. B. Simpson. The Wife or Love Stands (n.p., n.d.), 25. The important contribution of Simpson's associate and biographer A. E. Thompson to the promotion of Zionist views in late nineteenth-century evangelical circles is well discussed in David A. Rausch, Zionism Within Early American Fundamentalism, 1878–1918 (New York and Toronto: Edwin Mellen Press, 1979), 118–21.

[17]W. M. Turnbull, The Shadow of the Sun-Dial or the Destiny of the Jew (New York: Christian Alliance, n.d.), 3.

an international holiness and healing conference convened at Liverpool, England, in 1885, Simpson lucidly expounded the process by which the "Fourfold Gospel," once lost, was being restored gradually to the church:

> We want it all; we want the dead Christ; we want the risen Christ; we want the reigning Christ! And we say this Glorious Gospel is no new thing. God's Word was buried for centuries, and we sometimes think that when Luther came, he gave us back all the Gospel, but that was what we had no right to expect. He gave us part of it; he gave us justification by faith. He pulled out the telescope of divine revelation one length, and that was all. Then came those blessed men, the leaders of the revival in Germany and England, the men who brought in the Gospel of regeneration and the Holy Ghost—men like Locke and Whitfield [sic]. These men pulled out another length of the telescope, and then came others who taught us to expect mighty things of God, and to look to the real fulfillment of His promises, and then came this blessed hope, of Christ's coming as if emerging from the ashes of centuries. And then came the gospel of divine healing. I have read it in the life of George Whitfield. Anyone who read that life with care will find it, also in the writings of John Wesley, and in the great Church of England Prayer-book of Edward VI, where I have often read it. It is found also in the lives of German leaders. It is no new thing; it is the old Gospel of the Apostolic Church come back again (glory be to God). And we are only beginning to open it.[18]

Simpson's doctrine of a progressive historical revelation of lost truth led him to assert that

> from age to age God speaks the special message most needed so that there is always some portion of Divine truth which might properly be called present truth, God's message to the times.[19]

The responsibility for intuiting and proclaiming the divine plan for a specific time fell to the "prophet," whom Simpson described as "not so much a teacher of the written Word as a messenger of the very thing that God would say at the time to the generation to which he speaks or the community to whom he bears witness." The prophetic ministry, though embracing the task of teaching, remains unique in the sense that it calls for an "immediate power

---

[18]*Thy Healer* 2 (1885): 217–18. Essentially the same thesis is set forth in Simpson, *Present Truth*, 5–7.

[19]Simpson, *Present Truth*, 6–7.

and unction of the Holy Spirit" to enable the prophet to discern "the mind of his Master" and dispense it "to his fellowmen at the divine direction."[20] In this respect, Simpson saw himself functioning in a "prophetic" capacity. On occasions he regarded even some of his dreams as divinely sent to confirm new directions he was to undertake.[21]

The restorationist view of church history adhered to by Simpson and other contemporaries was chronologically extended by early Pentecostals to rationalize their distinctive claim that they had recovered the full apostolic baptism of the Holy Spirit accompanied by speaking in tongues. In variant forms, restorationism has survived in the twentieth century as an essential ingredient of the Pentecostal and neo-Pentecostal apologetic.[22]

Simpson's Doctrine of the Baptism of the Holy Spirit

Historians have made various attempts at locating precisely Simpson's theology of the baptism of the Holy Spirit within the contours of late nineteenth-century holiness movements. He has been variously identified with the views of R. A. Torrey, C. I. Scofield,[23] the Oberlin perfectionism of Asa Mahan and W. E.

---

[20]Simpson, *The Apostolic Church* (Nyack and New York: Christian Alliance, n.d.), 138–39; cf. Simpson's article, "Gifts and Grace," CMAW 27 (June 29, 1907): 303, in which he distinguished prophecy from the teaching of doctrine on the basis that "the prophetic message has more immediate reference to the particular condition of the hearer and the need of immediate spiritual help." Thus Simpson saw all preaching as needing to have a "prophetic" thrust.

[21]See Simpson's description of two dreams from which he received guidance pertinent to his missionary vision and his "life of faith" in SS, 231. The precise dating of the dreams is problematic.

[22]See David A. Womack, *The Wellsprings of the Pentecostal Movement* (Springfield, Mo.: Gospel Publishing House, 1968), 83, who likens the relationship between the holiness movement and Pentecostalism to that between John the Baptist and Jesus Christ. Cf. the essay by the American Presbyterian charismatic theologian J. Rodman Williams, "A New Era in History," in J. Rodman Williams, *The Pentecostal Reality* (Plainfield, N.J.: Logos International, 1971), 46–47, and the writings of the Church of England and British Methodist charismatics in Michael Harper, *As at the Beginning* (Plainfield, N.J.: Logos International, 1971), 22; and Leslie Davison, *Pathway to Power: The Charismatic Movement in Historical Perspective* (Watchung, N.J.: Charisma Books, 1972), 77f.

[23] Harold D. Hunter, *Spirit-Baptism: A Pentecostal Alternative* (Lanham: University of America Press, 1983), 189.

Boardman in the tradition of Charles Finney,[24] a Keswick-type concept of christocentric sanctification (as opposed to the Wesleyan eradicationist view of holiness),[25] and the theology of "Reformed evangelicals" such as A. J. Gordon and A. T. Pierson, who dissociated themselves from the Wesleyan holiness movement by "[denying] that sanctification was instantaneous . . . and [contending] that sanctification was not the baptism with the Holy Spirit."[26] In fact, the pluralist nature of Simpson's views on this subject makes efforts to classify them virtually useless.

Notwithstanding the difficulty in accurately contextualizing Simpson, the entire corpus of his writings testifies uniformly to his understanding of the baptism of the Holy Spirit (also termed "second blessing," "crisis sanctification," "the anointing," "the sealing," "receiving the Holy Spirit," "the indwelling of Christ") as a necessary experience in the life of the believer subsequent to and distinct from conversion-regeneration. Paramount for the believer is the example of Christ. Simpson held that, as an infant, Christ had been born of the Spirit but "not baptized with the Spirit until His thirtieth year" when he underwent water baptism in the Jordan River at the hands of John the Baptist.[27] This enduement with power, bringing to an end Christ's "quiet years in Nazareth," was indispensable to Jesus' earthly ministry, which Simpson interpreted as being accomplished in the power of Spirit-filled humanity.[28] Just as Jesus "received the Holy Ghost into His own person and for three and a half years walked through Galilee and Judea *in the Spirit*'" (Simpson's emphasis), so Christ imparts a personal baptism with the Holy Spirit to each expectant believer.[29] Simpson's establishment of the identity between Christ

---

[24]Donald R. Wheelock, "Spirit Baptism in American Pentecostal Thought" (Ph.D. diss., Emory University, 1983), 51f., esp. 56.

[25]William W. Menzies, "The Non-Wesleyan Origins of the Pentecostal Movement," in *Aspects of Pentecostal-Charismatic Origins*, ed. Vinson Synan (Plainfield, N.J.: Logos International, 1975), 87f.

[26]Edith L. Waldvogel (Blumhofer), "The 'Overcoming' Life: A Study in the Reformed Evangelical Contribution to Pentecostalism," *Pneuma* 1 (Spring 1979): 8–9.

[27]A. B. Simpson, "The Baptism of the Holy Spirit, a Crisis or an Evolution," LT 5 (December 1905): 705.

[28]A. B. Simpson: *Walking in the Spirit* (1889; reprint, Harrisburg: Christian Publications, n.d.), 7, 64; *Power from on High*, 2:14, 15, 20; *The Gospel of Luke*, Christ in the Bible Series (Harrisburg: Christian Publications, n.d.), 14b:38–45.

[29]See Simpson's discussion of Christ "The Baptizer," in A. B.

and the believer in the experience of Spirit baptism was anchored in a Christology that interwove the dual themes of the genuine humanity of Christ and the work of the Holy Spirit in the incarnate Christ, without falling prey to the ancient heresy of adoptionism. Ironically, earlier in the nineteenth century, a Christology with marked similarity to Simpson's had been controversially propounded by another Presbyterian preacher, Edward Irving. Though deposed as a minister of the Church of Scotland in 1833, partially on account of propagating an alleged christological heresy, Irving has more recently been rehabilitated as the "first Reformed-Pentecostal theologian."[30]

To Simpson, the exemplary value of Christ's being baptized with the Spirit was further substantiated in the lives of other New Testament characters. In the case of Christ's disciples, he described them as "undoubtedly saved men and women" prior to Pentecost, who as a result of their Spirit baptism at Pentecost underwent "an entirely new experience involving not only power for service, but power for holiness and righteousness in their own lives."[31] Overlooking the significance of the events in Judas's house (Acts 9:11–19), Simpson chose instead Romans 7–8 as the biblical proof for Paul's crisis experience subsequent to his conversion and posited Arabia rather than Damascus as the site where this occurred.[32] In this instance he was possibly influenced by the exegesis of George Pardington, a professor and theologian at the Nyack Missionary Training Institute who saw the events of Acts 9:17–18 as not "altogether clear" regarding the time of Paul's conversion and reception of the Holy Spirit.[33]

Simpson employed a variety of images to reinforce the import of the baptism of the Holy Spirit in one's spiritual life. He

---

Simpson, *The Names of Jesus* (New York: Christian Alliance, 1892), 240–70, esp. 244–45.

[30]See Gordon Strachan, *The Pentecostal Theology of Edward Irving* (Peabody, Mass.: Hendrickson, reprint, 1988), 13–22, and esp. 25–98, for a discussion of the pertinent christological themes.

[31]Simpson, "Baptism," LT 5 (December 1905): 709.

[32]Ibid., 715; Simpson, *Romans*, Christ in the Bible Series (New York: Christian Alliance, 1904), 17:149–84.

[33]See George P. Pardington, "The Crisis of the Deeper Life," LT 6 (September 1906): 536–37. He later concluded that Paul's case of receiving the Holy Spirit and being filled with the Spirit prior to water baptism was clearly the only instance of its kind in the New Testament (Pardington, "The Conversion of Paul," CMAW 32 [April 3, 1909]: 9).

likened it to an initiation into "the second year or chapter of [one's] spiritual history," the climax of salvation, or crossing the Jordan River and entering the promised land.[34] This special visitation of the Spirit comes about only as a result of "deep and intense desire," waiting upon God in sustained prayer and consecrating oneself unreservedly to the service of the Lord.[35] Waiting for the fullness of the Spirit could not be short-circuited. It was to Simpson "a discipline of self-crucifixion and stillness" without which there would be no "deep and full" reception of the Spirit.[36]

Most significantly, the baptism of the Holy Spirit was for Simpson the occasion at which the Spirit, who is present with the believer at conversion-regeneration, becomes fully resident "within the converted heart" and transforms it into "the temple of the Holy Ghost."[37] This crisis not only meets the "deeper need of sanctification" but also holds the secret of holiness and happiness.[38] In this experience the Holy Spirit becomes both "refiner" and "energizer."[39] Out of this experience flows the power to manifest holy character, supernatural gifts, and divine healing; the capacity to receive divine guidance and to endure suffering in the service of Christ; and the authority for governing the church.[40] The

---

[34]See the meditation for the ninth day in Simpson, *When the Comforter Came* (Harrisburg: Christian Publications, 1911); cf. idem, "Baptism," LT 5 (December 1905): 714; "The Ministry of the Spirit," LT 7 (August 1907): 440. I agree with Gerald McGraw's conclusion that Simpson "saw many deeper-life terms as practically interchangeable although theoretically differing in emphasis" ("Sanctification," 332).

[35]See the meditation for the thirtieth day in Simpson, *Comforter*; cf. idem, *Power from on High*, 2:67–76.

[36]Simpson, *The Christ of the Forty Days* (New York: Christian Alliance, n.d.), 233.

[37]Simpson, "Ministry of the Spirit," LT 7 (August 1907): 440: "The regenerated soul has the Holy Spirit with it, but not in it, even as the builder of a house may have constructed it by his own hand, but he has not yet made it his residence and his home"; cf. idem, "Baptism," LT 5 (December 1905): 707, 710; *Power from on High*, 2:50f. Simpson distinguished between the Spirit "with us," "in us," and "on us" as referring to the sequential experiences of: (1) converted but yet unsanctified; (2) consecrated and Spirit-baptized; (3) clothed with manifestations of the Spirit for the purpose of Christian service ("What is Meant by the Latter Rain," CMAW 29 [October 19, 1907]: 38).

[38]See the meditation for the twenty-ninth day in Simpson, *Comforter*.

[39]Simpson, *Power from on High*, 2:24f.

[40]On the multiple consequences of Spirit baptism, see Simpson: *Walking*, 101f.; *Forty Days*, 237f.; *Power from on High*, 2:77–89; *Apostolic Church*,

power of the Holy Spirit is given above all for a life of "the most strenuous service" and only secondarily for spiritual enjoyment.[41] Since it is this experience that transforms the "real . . . honest . . . constant church member" into one "possessed by the indwelling God," Simpson refused to exempt any person in the church, regardless of his or her role or position, from the need to be baptized with the Holy Spirit:

> The mother needs it in the nursery, the Sunday School teacher in his class, the preacher in his pulpit, the soul winner in his dealings with the inquirer, and the saint in his ministry of prayer in the secret closet.[42]

Simpson's concern to draw attention to the baptism of the Holy Spirit was heightened by a sense of prophetic urgency. In a 1906 editorial he declared the baptism of the Holy Spirit to be the "greatest thought that God [was] projecting upon the hearts of Christians," during what he perceived as a time of "increasing revival."[43] As a restorationist, Simpson laid much of the blame for the loss of this important truth at the feet of the sixteenth-century Protestant Reformers. Though he rediscovered justification by faith, Luther nevertheless "failed to go on to the deeper teachings of the Christian life," thereby consigning Germany to a "cold and lifeless rationalism and all its attendant evils."[44] In contrast, the religious life of England and America was decisively shaped by the inspired personalities of Wesley, Baxter, Whitefield, Moody, and Gordon, who knew well and preached concerning the ministry of the Holy Spirit.[45]

Simpson's espousal of a normative two-step pattern of Christian initiation, biblically legitimized by the experience of Christ, the apostles, and the early church, dictated his trenchant opposition to any doctrine of progressive sanctification which

---

163; *The Acts of the Apostles*, Christ in the Bible Series (Harrisburg: Christian Publications, n.d.), 16:124, 39.

[41]Simpson, *The Cross of Christ*, 130.

[42]Simpson, *Present Truth*, 138; cf. Simpson, *The Fullness of Jesus*, 65, 66.

[43]Simpson, "Editorial," LT 6 (March 1906): 129.

[44]Simpson, *The Four-fold Gospel* (1887; reprint, Harrisburg: Christian Publications, 1925), 28.

[45]Ibid., 28–29; Simpson, *Earnests of the Coming Age* (New York: Christian Alliance, 1921), 24–25. For further comment on the imperfections and limited success of the Protestant Reformation, see also Simpson, *The Land of Promise* (New York: Christian Alliance, 1888), 257; "Editorial," WWW 5 (1885): 13.

undermined the importance of a Spirit baptism subsequent to conversion-regeneration. He grouped together those "progressivists," including the reputable Keswick speaker F. B. Meyer, who minimized the necessity of a post-regeneration Spirit baptism, with the Darwinian "evolutionists," who explained the earth's history in terms of a process of natural development devoid of any catastrophic divine intervention.[46] Simpson insisted that the baptism of the Spirit, even if following almost immediately after conversion-regeneration, was nevertheless distinctive:

> We are willing, however, to concede that the baptism of the Holy Ghost may be received at the very same time a soul is converted. We have known a sinner to be converted, sanctified and saved all within a single hour, and yet each experience was different in its nature and was received in proper order and by a definite faith for that particular blessing.[47]

There was, in Simpson's words, no need for a "long interval" between conversion-regeneration and the baptism of the Holy Spirit. In the early church, the two events, though distinguishable, were either "contemporaneous or close together."[48]

Not to be misconstrued as a terminal point in the believer's spiritual journey, Spirit baptism, as promoted by Simpson, introduces Christians into a life of repeated baptisms, which take them ever deeper into the incomprehensible fullness of God. He taught that in the Spirit-filled life, there are "Pentecosts and second Pentecosts . . . great freshlets and flood-tides" that punctuate the ongoing process of receiving divine life "breath by breath and moment by moment."[49] In observing the church calendar, Simpson set apart the days following the celebration of Easter as the most appropriate season for seeking "a deeper filling, a mightier baptism" of the Holy Spirit, through a personal reenactment of the apostles' tarrying for the first Pentecost.[50] Under no illusions about the limitations of "crisis experiences,"

---

[46]Simpson: "Baptism," LT 5 (December 1905): 705, 707; "The Crisis of the Deeper Life," LT 6 (September 1906): 520–21; cf. "Editorial," CMAW 24 (May 27, 1905): 321, for a criticism of Meyer's progressivism, which taught sanctification as evolving out of regeneration.

[47]Simpson, "Baptism," LT 5 (December 1905): 707.

[48]Simpson, "Crisis," LT 6 (September 1906): 523.

[49]Simpson, A Larger Christian Life (New York: Christian Alliance, 1890), 81; cf. Simpson, Walking, 133.

[50]Simpson, Cross, 130.

he warned against the serious consequences of backsliding after being baptized in the Spirit. Unless believers persistently culti-vated a separated and consecrated life, Simpson deemed it all too possible to regress from "even . . . the very . . . deepest and highest experiences of the Holy Ghost."[51]

From the time of his own baptism of the Holy Spirit in 1874 during his second pastorate in Louisville, Kentucky, until his death in 1919, Simpson consistently upheld and defended the doctrine of a post-regeneration Spirit baptism. For him, this was a strategic, non-negotiable, doctrinal tenet of the Alliance. He was, however, tolerant of the various holiness traditions of inter-preting the theological and practical implications of the experi-ence of Spirit baptism. In reality, Simpson's Alliance embraced within its fellowship persons who represented all variations of the late nineteenth-century holiness movement, including "eradi-cationists" and "suppressionists," provided they did not engage militantly other views of sanctification held within the organiza-tion. Such de facto pluralism led him to conclude that it was unrealistic to expect "that all the teachers of sanctification could agree about phases and phrases."[52] He considered a dogmatism of experience and/or creed to be equally injurious to the unity of his organization. Hence, Simpson pursued a policy of diversity within unity on the matter of the baptism of the Holy Spirit, a policy that in time also allowed for the Pentecostal alternative view of Spirit baptism but not its exclusivist doctrine of initial evidence (tongues speech is the sole evidence of Spirit baptism). Even after the Pentecostal controversy had reached its peak in Alliance circles, the preservation of the doctrine and experience of Spirit baptism following conversion-regeneration remained a crucial concern for Simpson. As late as 1913 he charged that due to the pervasive influence of evolutionary theory, the doctrine of "a spiritual crisis after conversion, followed by entire consecra-tion and the baptism of the Holy Spirit," was "becoming obsolete . . . in evangelical religious circles."[53]

---

[51]Simpson, *Land of Promise*, 226f.; cf. idem, *Danger Lines in the Deeper Life* (New York: Christian Alliance, 1898), 7–9.

[52]Simpson, "Editorial," LT 6 (February 1906): 132; cf. AR (1908–09), 40; Simpson, "Editorial," CMAW 30 (August 1, 1908): 296; "Side Issues and the Supreme Object of Life," CMAW 30 (September 19, 1908): 416, on the assort-ment of "holiness" mentors esteemed by the rank and file of his followers.

[53]Simpson, "Editorial," AW 39 (March 1, 1913): 337.

Simpson's Views on the Gifts of the Holy Spirit

Like many of his evangelical associates Simpson expected the present age to conclude with the days of the "latter rain," when there would be a "special outpouring of the Holy Spirit upon the world," resulting in the conversion of "great multitudes." Whereas the day of Pentecost had marked the coming of the "early rain," Simpson discerned the "latter rain" as falling in his own time. To substantiate this conjecture, he appealed both to the success of revivalists of Europe and America in the closing decades of the nineteenth century and to the large strides taken by Protestant missionary organizations around the world. This unprecedented advance of the gospel on foreign fronts signaled to Simpson that the "bride" was being prepared for the soon coming of the "bridegroom."[54]

Simpson, in his various publications, frequently alluded to the eschatological significance of the Joel 2 prophecy. The "latter rain," which had already begun to "sprinkle" in his own time, would continue to intensify as the second advent approached, reaching proportions never before witnessed in church history.[55] From the fact that the "early rain" had come at Pentecost accompanied by supernatural manifestations of the Spirit such as tongues, miracles, and prophecy, Simpson deduced that one could rightly expect these "wonderful manifestations" to be part and parcel of the "latter rain."[56] Believers were urged to pray for "a special manifestation of the supernatural power of God," since this had typified the great revivals of the past.[57] Moreover, for the church to attain "full maturity" prior to Christ's return, it must be "adorned with all the gifts and graces of her divine ministry."[58] For the Spirit to complete his work of

---

[54]See Simpson, *The Gospel of the Kingdom*, 214; Simpson, *The Coming One*, 190–91; cf. his meditations for the twenty-fifth and twenty-sixth days of the month in *Comforter* and his poem, "The Latter Rain," in Simpson, *Songs of the Spirit* (New York: Christian Alliance, 1920), 52.

[55]See Simpson's editorials: "The Latter Rain," LT 6 (September 1906): 519; "Editorial," CMAW 34 (February 4, 1905): 65; "Editorial," CMAW 27 (June 8, 1907): 205; "What is Meant by the Latter Rain," CMAW 29 (October 19, 1907): 38; cf. "A Great Revival," CMAW 30 (September 26, 1908): 431.

[56]Simpson, "Editorial," LT 6 (December 6, 1906): 706; "Spiritual Sanity," LT 7 (April 1907): 191.

[57]Simpson, "Editorial," CMAW 24 (April 8, 1905): 209.

[58]Simpson, "Editorial," LT 7 (August 1907): 433.

preparing the church for Christ's appearance, believers must not fear him, but rather seek to understand fully his person and work. Only then would they be "ready to cooperate with Him and receive all His gifts and graces."[59]

A logical corollary of Simpson's doctrine of the "latter rain" and his restorationism was his categorical rejection of cessationism. Cessationism, promoted by churchmen of varying ecclesiastical stripes, contended that the supernatural gifts of the Spirit had by divine intention ceased with the end of the apostolic age.[60] Given his commitment to advance the cause of divine healing through involvement with an interdenominational, internationally based healing movement, Simpson found cessationism especially objectionable. Moreover, he saw no biblical grounds for drawing a dispensational distinction between the apostolic and later periods of church history, since the Pentecostal promise of Joel 2 and Paul's discussion of spiritual gifts in 1 Corinthians 12 affirm the continued presence of supernatural gifts of the Holy Spirit in the church until the second advent.[61] In his first published work, *The King's Business* (1886), Simpson upheld the early church with its dependence on spiritual gifts as the ever-relevant model for a supernaturally empowered Christian ministry. The "charismata" or spiritual gifts listed in 1 Corinthians and "clearly recognized" in the apostolic era properly belong to "the church of Christ through the whole Christian age."[62] Far from teaching their having ceased, Simpson avowed that the "various gifts of knowledge, wisdom, faith, miracles, healing, prophecy, tongues . . . [and] discerning of Spirits" were "designed to be zealously sought, cherished and cultivated" by Christians.[63] The ongoing manifestation of spiritual gifts in an ecclesial context was theologized by Simpson as a continuation of the resurrection life of Christ.[64] He denounced the cessationist theory as "one of the lies the devil [had] sugar-coated, candied and crystallized in the form of a theological

---

[59]Simpson, "Gifts and Grace," CMAW 27 (June 29, 1907): 303; cf. Simpson, "The Ministry of the Spirit," LT 7 (August 1907): 438.

[60]For example, see Jon Ruthven, "On the Cessation of the Charismata: The Protestant Polemic of Benjamin B. Warfield," *Pneuma* 12 (Spring 1990): 14–31.

[61]Simpson, *Healing*, 51–52.

[62]Simpson, *The King's Business* (New York: Word, Work and World, 1886), 335.

[63]Ibid., 335–36.

[64]Ibid., 336–37.

maxim."[65] Such a deception could not be endorsed by any Spirit-filled Christian because "the dear Master never contemplated or proposed any post-apostolic gulf of impotence and failure."[66]

Simpson argued that "unbelief and sin" in the church, and not divine volition, were the real culprits in the declining appearance of spiritual gifts after the death of the apostles.[67] Citing the church fathers Irenaeus and Tertullian as authorities, he posited that the supernatural gifts of the Spirit had continued in the post-apostolic church as late as the fifth century, wherever "faith and holiness" were retained in some measure.[68] The recovery of divine healing logically implied the continuation of "all the *charismata* of the Pentecostal Church," including the gift of tongues, which had been present throughout the history of the church.[69] Every generation of Christians needed "a living Christ" to perform miracles that authenticated the gospel in the face of unbelievers. The necessity of signs and wonders had certainly not diminished since the close of the apostolic era—if anything the need for the supernatural had only escalated in modern times:

> We are in the age of miracles, the age of Christ, the age which lies between two Advents . . . the age of Power, the age which, above all other ages of time, should be intensely alive. . . . Until he [Christ] comes again, the world will never cease to need the touch of His Power and Presence in the form of supernatural spiritual manifestations.[70]

Simpson insisted that just as the preaching of the gospel in the book of Acts had been "sealed . . . with signs and wonders" so the church had "a right to expect such manifestations in every new stage of Christian work today."[71] He had biting words for those churches in which supernatural gifts of the Holy Spirit were absent, calling them "religious club[s] bound together by social affinities," and only "moderately exercised and occupied in respectable forms of benevolence and usefulness."[72] He suggested

---

[65]Simpson, *Earnests*, 118.

[66]Simpson, *Healing*, 52.

[67]Ibid., 53.

[68]Ibid., 54.

[69]See Simpson's dependence on the longer ending of Mark 16 as proof of the permanence of healing and tongues in *Healing*, 59.

[70]Ibid., 55, 57.

[71]Simpson, *Forty Days*, 252.

[72]Simpson, *Apostolic Church*, 133.

satirically that in such churches, biblical "exegesis" actually meant "exit Jesus."[73]

More seriously, Simpson warned that a church devoid of the supernatural powers of the Holy Spirit would be defenseless against the false miracles of Satan in the end times.[74] The growing popularity of Darwinism and the "higher criticism" of the Bible mirrored the "increasing rationalism" and "unbelief" of the age.[75] Lamentably, the Darwinian theory of natural "development," which Simpson punned as "devilment,"[76] had seduced the church, causing even the clergy to attempt to purge the supernatural from both the Scriptures and the church. He chided those of the clergy who preferred to search for reductionist explanations of supernatural phenomena rather than to endorse and open themselves to the miraculous working of God.[77]

On the issue of naturalism versus supernaturalism the lines were clearly drawn for Simpson. As history progressed toward its apocalyptic climax, he prophesied a steadily mounting confrontation between the "manifestations of divine power" identified with the "latter rain" and the forces of rationalism and materialism that fastened their grip on Western civilization.[78] Consequently he summoned the "minister[s] of the Lord" to "claim" and "exercise" in the power of the Holy Spirit the "gifts and offices" given to them. He exhorted them never to accommodate themselves placidly to the antisupernaturalistic sentiments of the age, but rather to remain vigilant and seek more discernment in spiritual matters, thereby arousing the church from its alleged slumber.[79]

Simpson's Use of the Book of Acts

Simpson's interpretation of the book of Acts was not essentially different from that of the modern Pentecostal move-

---

[73]Simpson, *Forty Days*, 242.

[74]Simpson, *Healing*, 54–55.

[75]Ibid., 70–71; cf. Simpson's critique of Darwinism and biblical higher criticism as opponents of a supernaturalist worldview in *Old Faith*, 9–57.

[76]Simpson, *Earnests*, 15.

[77]Simpson: *Walking*, 140; *Apostolic Church*, 133.

[78]Simpson, *Walking*, 140.

[79]Simpson, *Healing*, 73–74.

ment, which sees in Acts a representation of normal church life as God intended it to be throughout all periods of church history. He was, as are Pentecostals, fully prepared to employ the standard of spiritual life portrayed in Acts as the experiential norm by which to measure the shortcomings of the church in his own time. He believed that the entire book expounds the supernatural quality of the Christian life that becomes evident when the church abides in the fullness of the Holy Spirit. Apart from the ongoing release of the power of the Holy Spirit in apostolic fashion, Simpson insisted that the church would inevitably substitute a "conventional formalism" for genuine Christian work.[80]

The writings of Simpson indicate clearly that he anticipated the Pentecostal hermeneutical practice of deriving doctrine from the narrative accounts of Acts. This exegetical method, which assumed the didactic value of history, contributed in no small way to Simpson's theology of the ministry of the Holy Spirit in the life of the believer that sought to legitimize a two-step model of Christian initiation—conversion-regeneration and Spirit baptism. Despite his rejection of the "initial evidence" doctrine, which Pentecostals attempted to defend from Acts, Simpson drew heavily from some of the later classical proof texts of Pentecostalism (Acts 2, 8, 19) to build the case for conversion-regeneration and Spirit baptism as two distinct, sequential events in the *ordo salutis* of the believer.

For him, as for Pentecostals, the Acts of the Apostles demonstrates that the reception of the Holy Spirit in fullness occurs subsequent to conversion-regeneration. Just as the apostles waited in the upper room to receive the "baptism of power," so all believers are to follow the apostolic example of tarrying. The apostles, Simpson explained, needed to wait for the Spirit not only from the standpoint of the eschatological fulfillment of the divine purpose on the Feast of Pentecost, according to the Hebrew calendar, but also out of psychological necessity. They needed to "search their hearts [and] deepen the hunger and the longing which were necessary for them to appreciate the blessing."[81] The historical precedent was thus established for future converts who had "accepted Jesus" to be instructed immediately upon their conversion as to how to receive the Holy Spirit. Pre-

---

[80]Simpson, *Present Truth*, 148; cf. Simpson, *Acts*, 447.
[81]Simpson, *Acts*, 23–24.

scribing a pastoral methodology for dealing with seekers, Simpson advised:

> so still [after conversion] we should lead the convert to the altar of consecration, and never leave him until he has been sealed and sanctified by the same Spirit.[82]

Regarding the experience of the Samaritans in Acts 8, he commented that after embracing the "testimony of Jesus" through the evangelistic ministry of Philip, they received subsequently a "personal baptism of the Holy Ghost" at the hands of the apostolic delegation from Jerusalem.[83] The same two-step pattern of initiation was repeated in the case of the Ephesian disciples in Acts 19. For Simpson, these converts of John the Baptist typified "a great majority of professing Christians" in his own time who had been converted but who "[had] not received the Holy Ghost" and "[made] no claim to sanctification."[84] The question posed by Paul to the Ephesians, "Have ye received the Holy Ghost since ye believed?" could equally be asked of many contemporary churchgoers who knew only the "ministry of repentance."[85]

From the biographical data on Apollos in Acts 18, Simpson derived "Lessons in the Higher Christian Life." He proposed that Apollos represented the impoverished condition of "hundreds and thousands of ministers and Christians" who had never progressed beyond repentance and conversion-regeneration.[86] Only after being led into the deeper Christian life by Aquila and Priscilla did Apollos receive a "new theology," a "new experience," and a "new equipment" for Christian work.[87]

---

[82]Ibid., 49; cf. Simpson's interpretation of Acts 2:38 as teaching that baptism with the Holy Spirit follows repentance and water baptism (ibid., 43, 123).

[83]Simpson: Forty Days, 252–53; Acts, 54–55.

[84]Simpson, Acts, 122.

[85]Ibid., 123, 120. Simpson's exegesis and application of these texts in Acts does not differ essentially from that of numerous Pentecostal and charismatic writers. For recent examples, see J. Rodman Williams, The Gift of the Holy Spirit Today (Plainfield, N.J.: Logos International, 1980); Howard M. Ervin, Conversion-Initiation and the Baptism in the Holy Spirit (Peabody, Mass.: Hendrickson, 1984); Roger Stronstad, The Charismatic Theology of St. Luke (Peabody, Mass.: Hendrickson, 1984); and Stanley M. Horton, The Book of Acts (Springfield, Mo.: Gospel Publishing House, 1981).

[86]Simpson, In the School of Christ (New York: Christian Alliance, 1890), 211; cf. Simpson, Acts, 120.

[87]Simpson, School, 215–16.

In this context, Simpson castigated the established church for its "intellectual self-sufficiency" and overdependence upon "colleges and books," all of which were impotent to convey the quality of life lived in the fullness of the Holy Spirit. A "cold and worldly church" invariably had an overabundance of Apollos' followers but a tragic lack of truly "anointed messengers" capable of leading others into "a life of consecration and full salvation."[88] From the example of Apollos, Simpson drew pointed conclusions regarding the indispensability of the baptism of the Holy Spirit to the spiritual well-being of the church:

> The general lesson from the life of Apollos is the necessity of a real spiritual experience of the deeper things of God and a baptism of the Holy Ghost, if we would be used effectually in the work of God. . . . The church today is suffering from too much intellectual culture and too little spiritual unction. No class of men more than the class represented by Apollos need the baptism of the Holy Ghost. The more brain we have, the more spiritual power we need to preserve the true balance of humility and heavenly mindedness.[89]

In his work *Forward Movements of the Last Half Century* (1905), Arthur T. Pierson, a prominent Presbyterian minister, called the "Pentecostal movement," with its emphasis on receiving the Pentecostal gift of the Spirit for "sanctifying, enduring, and filling," the most important of the "spiritual movements" of the later nineteenth century.[90] Simpson was one of many within the world of nineteenth-century evangelical Protestantism who came to reject the historicist interpretation of Pentecost because it defined the importance of the event solely in terms of introducing a new dispensation of the Holy Spirit. Not denying the historical uniqueness of Pentecost, he also saw the various effusions of the Spirit recounted in Acts as constituting a pattern for a normative "Pentecost" to be appropriated personally by all believers since New Testament days, just like the sacrifice of Christ for the forgiveness of sins. The collective experience of Christ and the first generation of Christians apparently corroborated Simpson's own doctrine and spiritual journey which highlighted the Pentecostal gift of the Spirit not as the automatic consequence of conversion-

---

[88]Ibid., 214, 217, 218.
[89]Ibid., 222, 223.
[90]Arthur T. Pierson, *Forward Movements of the Last Half Century* (1905; reprint, New York and London: Garland, 1984), 137.

regeneration but as the rightful inheritance of those who sought for it subsequent to their initial faith in Christ. To Simpson, an analogy between the experience of the Spirit in the lives of Christ, the apostles, and other first-century believers and that of Christians in the post-New Testament era was the exegetical cornerstone of his proclamation of a Spirit baptism subsequent to conversion-regeneration that lifted one to a higher plane of Christian living. This paradigmatic and didactic use of Lukan "Spirit" narratives in the New Testament foreshadowed a dominant strain of teaching on Spirit baptism in twentieth-century Pentecostalism and neo-Pentecostalism.[91]

------

[91] This dimension of neo-Pentecostal exegesis is thoroughly surveyed and assessed in H. I. Lederle, *Treasures Old and New. Interpretations of "Spirit-Baptism" in the Charismatic Renewal Movement* (Peabody, Mass.: Hendrickson, 1988), 55f. See evangelical Harold Lindsell's suggestion that Simpson "stressed certain doctrines commonly manifested in the charismatic movement" (*The Holy Spirit in the Latter Days* [Nashville: Nelson, 1983], 23). He also notes the "lasting impact" of Simpson and his revivalist contemporaries on "today's charismatics" (ibid., 24). For an interesting analysis of the need for non-Pentecostal scholars to acknowledge the hermeneutical legitimacy of Pentecostal approaches to Luke-Acts, see Ben Aker, "New Directions in Lucan Theology: Reflections on Luke 3:21–22 and Some Implications," in *Faces of Renewal*, ed. Paul Elbert (Peabody, Mass.: Hendrickson, 1988), 108–27.

YEARS OF EXPECTATION AND CRISIS: 1905–1912

A RECENT STUDY BY ALLIANCE PASTOR and historian Ernest G. Wilson refers to the incursion of Pentecostalism into the ranks of the Alliance during the first decade of this century as the "most serious crisis" and "the greatest problem" in Alliance history. Wilson also claims that the Alliance, as a result of "unhappy experiences with Pentecostal people," changed doctrinal camps in practice if not in theory, by diminishing its "active relationships" with "Pentecostal, charismatic or holiness groups" in favor of strengthening both its contacts with " 'Baptistic groups' and . . . emphasis on 'Baptistic' doctrinal concepts."[1] Simpson's response to Pentecostalism was conditioned both by his own spiritual journey and by the stress of having to deal with variant assessments of the movement by members of the Alliance. Many (some leaders included) received the Pentecostal baptism with tongues and had evident Pentecostal sympathies, while others were suspicious of, and strongly opposed to, the movement.[2]

---

[1] Ernest G. Wilson, "The Christian and Missionary Alliance: Developments and Modifications of Its Original Objectives" (Ph.D. diss., New York University, 1984), 374f.

[2] See Anderson, *Vision*, 145, who states that the Alliance suffered defections from both "extreme pro-Pentecostals" and "anti-Pentecostals." Facing this polarization of attitudes, Simpson was understandably reluctant to move in either direction for fear of increasing the exodus of people.

Simpson's Attitude toward the Gift of Tongues
Prior to Azusa Street

Simpson's critique of Pentecostalism proceeded from a wholehearted affirmation of the continued presence within the church of all the gifts of the Spirit. In a series of sermons preached in 1898, later published under the title *The Apostolic Church*, he expounded systematically the nature and purpose of each of the *charismata* catalogued in 1 Corinthians 12.[3] Basing his observatio on 1 Corinthians 12:7, Simpson concluded that every believer "ought" to be endowed with "some . . . manifestation of the Holy Ghost and some gift for Christian service" according to the sovereignty of the Holy Spirit.[4] As one effect of the baptism of the Holy Spirit, the diversity of these supernatural powers makes them all equally vital to the health of the church. In its public meetings the church is to welcome all manifestations of the Spirit, including prophecy and tongues, provided that the "order . . . reverence and decorum due to the house of God" are not violated.[5] Since the "gifts of power" were, for Simpson, "the jewels upon the robes of the Bride [the church]," it was inconceivable that they could be either discredited or prohibited in ecclesiastical life.[6]

As early as 1883, Simpson responded to critics who saw his stance on divine healing as implying also the continuance of tongues in the church by maintaining that this charism, despite its historic susceptibility to abuse, was not to be excluded from those spiritual gifts being restored in the end time. It would be "repeated" wherever "the church humbly claim[ed] it for the universal diffusion of the Gospel."[7] In 1892, when Alliance mission-

---

[3] Simpson, *Apostolic Church*, 135f.

[4] Simpson, "Gifts and Grace," 302; cf. idem, *Power from on High*, 2:123: "Our ministries are determined, in some measure, by our place in the body, by our environment, by the circumstances and providences amid which we are placed, by leadings, and natural instincts and preferences, and by the gifts both of nature and of grace."

[5] Simpson, *Apostolic Church*, 178f., esp. 179.

[6] Ibid., 151.

[7] Simpson, "The Gospel of Healing," WWW 3 (October 1883): 172. The 1915 revised edition of *The Gospel of Healing* replaced the last two lines from WWW 3 (October 1883): 172, with the following: "To a greater or less extent the gift of tongues has been continuous in the Church of Christ, and along with many counterfeits has undoubtedly been realized in the present generation." These changes were made as a result of Simpson's observa-

aries deliberated over whether seeking the gift of tongues was preferable to language study in foreign missionary service, Simpson, though he was skeptical that it would be given as a substitute for naturally acquired languages, did not discourage the faith of missionaries to receive it.[8]

In terms of appreciating the benefit of tongues in Christian experience, Simpson was remarkably enlightened as to its function in worship. In 1898, he described tongues as an expression of "lofty spiritual feeling" and exaltation that, though not always "intelligible," nonetheless testified in a unique fashion to the presence, guidance, and power of the Holy Spirit.[9] At the same time, Simpson was wary of the chaotic, emotional excesses that had accompanied the Irvingite phenomenon of tongues earlier in the century and transformed the gift from an expression of heavenly utterance into a cause of disgrace and confusion.[10]

There is no observable reluctance in Simpson's pre-1906 writings to recognize the value of the gift of tongues and to concede its rightful status as a manifestation of the Holy Spirit that could be expected to reappear at any time in the church's history. In his estimation it was indeed being revived in late nineteenth-century holiness circles.[11] He hastened, however, to delineate the inherent limitations of the gift as compared to other manifestations of the Spirit. It is a "showy gift," the "least honored" of all the supernatural powers with which the church was endued.[12] When exercised by the vain and ambitious, it is prone

---

tions of Pentecostalism. See *The Gospel of Healing*, rev. ed. (New York: Christian Alliance, 1915; original edition, 1887), 59.

[8] Simpson: "The Gift of Tongues," CAMW 8 (February 12, 1892): 98; "Editorial," CAMW 9 (October 7 and 14, 1892): 226, 227; cf. Simpson, *Apostolic Church*, 139, 172, 174–76; "Queries," CAFMW 10 (February 2, 1894): 13; "Editorial," CMAW 26 (November 17, 1906): 305; "Editorial," LT 6 (December 1906): 707.

[9] Simpson, *Apostolic Church*, 140; cf. Simpson, "Gifts and Grace," 303, where he says of tongues that it is "in some sense a real opening of the doors between the earthly and the heavenly."

[10] Simpson: "The Supernatural Gifts and Ministries of the Church," CAFMW 20 (January 19, 1898): 54; "The Worship and Fellowship of the Church," CAFMW 20 (February 9, 1898): 125, 126.

[11] Simpson, *Apostolic Church*, 140; cf. idem, "Editorial," CMAW 27 (February 2, 1907): 49.

[12] Simpson, *Apostolic Church*, 148; cf. idem, "Editorial," LT 7 (January 1907): 2–3, where Simpson ranks tongues and miracles as "subordinate to the simple and practical ministry of teaching and prophesying."

to abuse and thus, to a large extent, had been withdrawn in the early post-apostolic age.[13] Simpson could point to the destruction of the ministry of the promising Scottish preacher Edward Irving as a more recent tragic illustration of the ominous consequences of a preoccupation with tongues. History held a stern warning for all who would pretentiously seek after the gift.[14] For Simpson, miraculous signs and supernatural gifts, as potent as they were in combating the besetting materialism of the age, needed to be authenticated by a humble lifestyle, a reverence for and literal adherence to the Scriptures, and a holy life consistent with the character of Jesus. In his final analysis, personal "purity" makes a stronger impression on the world than "the power of . . . lives and works."[15]

Simpson's Response to Azusa Street

A survey of Alliance periodical literature for 1905–06, immediately prior to the beginning of meetings at the Azusa Street Mission in 1906, indicates that the subject of spiritual renewal was uppermost in Simpson's mind. From January 1905 to April 1906, Alliance magazines were replete with announcements of movings of the Spirit in Wales and various American cities, notably New York and Los Angeles.[16] These reports were accompanied by appeals to the Alliance constituency to unite with other believers in concerted prayer[17] for evangelism, sacrificial stewardship on the part of the wealthy, consecration of young people, and the supernatural power of healing.[18] Simpson's writing pulsated with the conviction that he stood at the threshold of a fresh interdenominational outpouring

---

[13]Simpson: *Apostolic Church*, 140; "The Gift of Tongues," CAMW 8 (February 12, 1892): 98.

[14]Simpson, *Apostolic Church*, 175.

[15]Simpson, "Faith and Fanaticism," CAFMW 20 (February 9, 1898): 132.

[16]See Simpson: "Editorial," CMAW 24 (January 14, 1905): 17; "Editorial," CMAW 24 (February 25, 1905): 117; "Editorial," CMAW 24 (March 4, 1905): 129; "Editorial," CMAW 24 (April 29, 1905): 269; "Editorial," CMAW 25 (April 14, 1906): 212.

[17]See Simpson: "Editorial," CMAW 24 (February 4, 1905): 65; "Editorial," CMAW 24 (February 11, 1905): 81; "Editorial," CMAW 24 (March 11, 1905): 145; "Editorial," CMAW 24 (April 1, 1905): 193.

[18]Simpson, "Editorial," CMAW 24 (April 8, 1905): 209.

of the Spirit.[19] He perceived that his organization, by this time almost two decades old, was waning in its evangelistic zeal, and thus he encouraged his workers to be on the alert for a needed revival in Alliance churches and branch ministries.[20]

Events at Azusa Street coincided with a pre-Council assembly of Alliance workers at Nyack in later May 1906, designed both to achieve consensus regarding those primary matters of doctrine on which Alliance unity depended and to identify secondary issues of belief where difference of opinion was permissible. A preconference statement drafted by Simpson, Henry Wilson, J. D. Williams, A. E. Funk, and F. H. Senft, which was sent to all official workers, reaffirmed allegiance to the Fourfold Gospel—Christ as Savior, Sanctifier, Healer, and Coming King. Significantly, the section on sanctification stressed the "distinct" nature of the baptism of the Holy Spirit as an experience subsequent to conversion-regeneration that equipped the believer for service and holy living as well as being the catalyst for a future "deeper filling of the Holy Spirit."[21] The document was noticeably silent, however, on the subject of spiritual gifts. During the preceding month, Simpson had written that such "special enduements [are not] really essential to the baptism of the Holy Spirit," which could be had "without any of the supernatural gifts."[22]

Simpson's comments on Azusa Street first appeared in a September 1906 issue of the *Christian Alliance Weekly*. Relying on secondhand information, he described the occurrence of tongues in Los Angeles as "a remarkable manifestation of spiritual power among earnest Christians in the West" consisting of both "known languages" and "unintelligible . . . incoherent speech."[23] As an

---

[19]See Simpson's references to the Alliance's need for and the growing worldwide occurrence of revival in "The Revival Wave," LT 6 (February 1906): 65–66; "Editorial," LT 6 (March 1906): 129, 130, 131.

[20]Simpson, "Editorial," CMAW 24 (March 18, 1905): 161.

[21]The conference was first announced in Simpson's "Editorial," CMAW 24 (December 30, 1905): 817; and subsequently in "Editorial," CMAW 25 (March 31, 1906): 185; and in "Editorial," CMAW 25 (May 19, 1906): 297; cf. Pardington, *Twenty-five Wonderful Years*, 44; Robert Ekvall et al., *After Fifty Years* (Harrisburg: Christian Publications, 1939), 25. The text of the preliminary statement for the "Conference For Prayer and Counsel Respecting Uniformity in the Testimony and Teaching of The Alliance, May 25–28, 1906," is available in the Canadian Bible College/Canadian Theological Seminary Archives, Regina, Saskatchewan.

[22]Simpson, "Editorial," LT 6 (April 1906): 198.

[23]Simpson: "Editorial," CMAW 26 (September 22, 1906): 177;

apostle of "balance" in the spiritual life, Simpson cautioned his readers to avoid the two extremes of fanaticism and credulity, on the one hand, and an ultraconservative reaction on the other, which refused to acknowledge "any added blessing" that might accompany an end-time visitation of the Holy Spirit. To him the spiritual integrity of Alliance people exhibited in months of fervent prayer for revival logically implied a genuine openness to whatever form the answer to that prayer might take.[24]

Simpson's discriminating approval of the Azusa Street meetings was in stark contrast to the vitriolic rhetoric typical of other holiness and fundamentalist leaders.[25] His charitable assessment of the beginnings of Pentecostalism in the midst of much hostile anti-Pentecostal criticism by religious and nonreligious observers alike was not overlooked by Pentecostals. In 1916, Bennett F. Lawrence, a charter member of the AG who authored the first history of the Pentecostal movement, commended Simpson as a notable example of one who endorsed the reemergence of miracles and the gift of tongues in modern times. Lawrence further remembered Simpson for his "favorable editorial comment" on the Azusa Street meetings, at a time when friends of the new movement were few.[26] As late as 1947, Simpson was applauded by AG historian Carl Brumback for his refusal to render a negative verdict on the entire Pentecostal movement because of the "extravagances and errors" of a minority of persons who lapsed doctrinally and/or morally. For Brumback, Simpson modeled the posture of a "man of God" who "saw what others either could not or would not see, viz., the presence of God" in the movement. The Alliance leader's evaluation was an example of fairness worthy of emulation by other critics.[27]

"Editorial," LT 6 (December 1906): 707. Simpson also referred to xenoglossa as "real missionary tongues" ("What is Meant by the Latter Rain," CMAW 29 [October 19, 1907]: 38), but not with the same utilitarian value as believed by the Pentecostal, Charles F. Parham. For Parham's view, see Goff, Fields White Unto Harvest, 77–79.

[24]Simpson, "Editorial," CMAW 26 (September 22, 1906): 177, 199.

[25]For a well-documented survey of the vicious polemic of holiness and fundamentalist leaders against the Azusa Street revival and Pentecostalism, see Anderson, Vision, 141–43; cf. Blumhofer, Assemblies, 1:183–95.

[26]Bennett F. Lawrence, The Apostolic Faith Restored (St. Louis: Gospel Publishing House, 1916), 87.

[27]Carl Brumback, What Meaneth This? (Springfield, Mo.: Gospel Publishing House, 1947), 102.

When Simpson made his first public assessment of Azusa Street in September 1906, he probably saw events there more as a regional expression of a rising tide of continental and world-wide revival than as the crystallization of a new movement deriving its energy from an experience of "Pentecost" at odds with his own teaching and expectation. News from there proved to be in tune with the spiritual stirrings on the campus of the Missionary Training Institute at Nyack during the last three months of 1906 that spread to the town itself and nearby communities.[28] David McDowell, a student at the Institute during the fall of 1906, vividly recalled the spiritual climate at the school:

> Being a student of the Christian and Missionary Alliance train-ing school located at Nyack on the Hudson, I returned to take up my studies in October [1906] and found a very sacred atmos-phere surrounding the entire school and a mighty spirit of prayer on the whole student body. This continued daily until the latter part of October when the desire and hunger for God became so strong that it seemed impossible for any work to be done. We felt that God must meet us or we could not go on any further. . . .
>
> One Sunday at noon prayers a young woman got up and made a confession which was followed by another and yet another. . . . The dining halls were practically deserted for three or four days, many of the students fasting continually. There was such a great hush and sense of the sacred presence of God in the place that one would notice the students walking on tiptoe through the halls. . . . Tears flowed freely and God moved mightily for a space of two or three weeks before any order could be resumed again. As it seemed to Dr. Simpson that the time had arrived when the students should return to their studies, we obeyed but with hungry aching hearts.[29]

---

[28]See Simpson, "Editorial," CMAW 26 (November 10, 1906): 289; cf. F. E. Marsh: "Revival in the Missionary Institute at South Nyack on Hudson," CMAW 26 (November 17, 1906): 316, 318; "The Overturning Work of the Spirit," CMAW 26 (November 24, 1906): 323f.; "The Emphasis of the Holy Spirit in the Revival at Nyack and New York," CMAW 26 (December 1, 1906): 338; Fred R. Bullen, "Among the Nyack Students," CMAW 26 (December 1, 1906): 363.

[29]As quoted in Stanley H. Frodsham, *With Signs Following* (Spring-field, Mo.: Gospel Publishing House, 1926), 47–48; cf. David McDowell, "I Remember," PE (March 1, 1964): 13; Mary E. Lewer, "50 Years of Pentecos-tal Blessing," PE (January 26, 1958): 7.

McDowell's account is corroborated by the 1907 (for 1906) report of the principal, W. C. Stevens. Stevens saw this "visitation of God's Spirit" as "the most signal and sacred feature of [the] year's history," though he acknowledged that it still fell short of the expected "climax of demonstration of enduement," which had "not yet come."[30]

At Simpson's Gospel Tabernacle in New York City, special week-night meetings were convened to provide additional opportunities for testimony, prayer, and confession. The outbreak of tongues in some of these meetings evoked a response from Simpson. Consistent with his pre-Azusa Street viewpoint on the gifts of the Spirit, he resisted any attempt to promote tongues as the necessary initial evidence of the baptism of the Holy Spirit.[31] By the close of the year, Simpson was addressing his congregation on the differences between "true . . . and false fire" and "fervor and fanaticism," in order to safeguard them against error.[32]

Simpson's ability to affirm the Azusa Street revival as one of a growing number of worldwide manifestations of the "latter rain" was rooted in an intense personal desire that he and the Alliance would similarly share in the much awaited end-time outpouring of the Holy Spirit. That the meetings were marked by manifestations of tongues did not prejudice Simpson's evaluation of them in view of both his previous insistence on the continuation of all the gifts of the Spirit (including tongues) within the church and his commitment to the appropriate expression of them within biblical guidelines. In many respects, the words of Florence Crawford, later the founder of the Pentecostal

---

[30]W. C. Stevens, "Report from the Missionary Training Institute," AR (1906–07): 77–78; cf. Simpson's mention of the " 'baptism' which came to [the] Institute in the early Autumn," in "Annual Report of President and General Superintendent of the Christian and Missionary Alliance," AR (1906–07): 5, 6–8. He alluded to it as a "profound awakening" that came with "great power" and "awful revelations" of sin ("Editorial," LT 6 [December 1906]: 706).

[31]Simpson, "Editorial," CMAW 26 (November 17, 1906): 305.

[32]On Sunday morning, December 9, 1906, Simpson preached to his Tabernacle congregation from Leviticus 9:24 and 10:1, 2. See his "Fervor and Fanaticism," CMAW 26 (December 22, 1906): 390. "True and False Fire" was also the theme of a Simpson sermon at the Rocky Springs Park, Lancaster, Penn., camp meeting in July 1907 at which twelve thousand people attended the closing sessions. During the convention many received Spirit baptism with tongues. See Simpson, "Notes from the Home Field," CMAW 28 (September 7, 1907): 116.

organization the Apostolic Faith (headquarters at Portland, Oregon), in 1907 were indicative of Simpson's own mind-set on the events of Azusa Street. Reflecting on the heightening of spiritual expectation and the proliferation of prayer groups in Los Angeles prior to the outbreak of the revival in 1906, Crawford stated:

> I was a Methodist and felt sure that the Spirit would be poured out upon us. Some of my friends were Baptists, Christian and Missionary Alliance and others. We all said: "surely God will pour out His Spirit on our own particular group."[33]

Pentecostalism Encounters the Alliance

During the years 1907–08, Pentecostalism made its maximum penetration into the Alliance. The tardiness in formulating an official response to the issues generated by the spread of Pentecostalism stemmed largely from the fact that the Alliance was still in the process of evolving into an independent holiness denomination. In 1907 the predominant character of the Alliance was that of an interdenominational, higher-life, and missions association, composed mostly of persons who also retained membership in regular churches. This loosely knit network militated against comprehensive definition in areas of doctrine and polity. Those churches which were affiliated with the Alliance enjoyed a large degree of autonomy, hence their vulnerability to Pentecostal persuasion. The organizational fluidity of the Alliance at the outset of the twentieth century was typical of a first-generation renewal movement. Its unity was derived more from an inner spiritual fraternity created by a common experience of Simpson's Fourfold Gospel than from an externally imposed political structure.

The first eyewitness reports of Azusa Street started to reach Alliance branches in the eastern United States in late 1906 and early 1907. Miss Ivey Campbell, who had returned from Los Angeles where she had received a Spirit baptism with tongues, was instrumental in leading Alliance persons into the same experience in Akron and Cleveland, Ohio. The local superintendent of the Ohio branch, W. A. Cramer, pieced together the events a few months later:

---

[33]Compiled by veteran members of the headquarters staff, A *Historical Account of the Apostolic Faith* (Portland, Oreg.: Apostolic Faith, 1965), 43.

The news began to come to us of the Pentecostal outpourings in California and the foreign fields and we began to plead for a similar wave of blessing to reach us as well. A card reached us at this time from our Brother McKinney, of Akron, announcing meetings in the South Street Mission, conducted by Sister Ivey Campbell, who had returned from Los Angeles in the experience of the Pentecostal baptism.[34]

He personally attended two of Campbell's meetings and testified as to his own quest and eventual experience of Spirit baptism in Cleveland, ten days later:

When but a few of our company were met together at the hall for prayer . . . the power of God fell on me and while prostrated upon the floor a new revelation of the glory of my risen Lord was granted me, and while in this condition the Holy Spirit took possession of my body and soon began to speak through me words in a language or utterance I had never learned nor heard before.[35]

As a result of Ivey Campbell's visit to Cleveland, where she conducted meetings for four weeks, Cramer reported that "possibly fifty persons" received "the baptism." Miraculous healings also attended the tongues speaking.[36]

The initial response of Alliance authorities to these Pentecostal phenomena in Ohio was unanimously supportive. Cramer, understandably, interpreted the events as a genuine outpouring of the Spirit which "continue[d] in a most modest and steady inflow."[37] According to his colleagues in the Ohio district, Cramer and the field chairman from New York, Dr. Henry Wilson,

were all in perfect accord with the testimony given by those who had received their Pentecost, and expressed themselves in thorough sympathy with the experiences as witnessed in our midst.[38]

Simpson concurred. In an editorial summary of Wilson's investigative trip to Ohio (done at Simpson's instigation), he reiterated his associate's conclusion that in the Ohio district

---

[34]W. A. Cramer, "Pentecost at Cleveland," CMAW 27 (April 27, 1907): 201.
[35]Ibid.
[36]Ibid.
[37]Ibid.
[38]Ibid.

there was "a deep spirit of revival" free from "fanaticism and excess."[39]

In January 1907, another participant in the Azusa Street meetings, Glenn A. Cook, related his experience of Spirit baptism to the Alliance branch in Indianapolis, Indiana, which aroused a desire for tarrying meetings.[40]

Unlike Ohio, however, events did not transpire smoothly. The superintendent, George N. Eldridge, while out of town, banned the tarrying meetings from the Alliance Tabernacle, and division ensued. Half of the members left and joined the Apostolic Faith movement.[41] By the time Simpson came to Indianapolis in June to preach at the summer convention, the split brought on by the controversy over tongues was irreversible.[42]

The frequency of manifestations of tongues steadily increased in Alliance gatherings during 1907. In his diary, Simpson noted that "several cases of the Gift of Tongues and other extraordinary manifestations" characterized meetings of the general council that convened at Nyack in May.[43] Most likely, all of the eight summer conventions witnessed tongues speaking, as a growing number of prominent Alliance persons received their Spirit baptisms.[44] Included among these were John Salmon, Mrs.

---

[39] See Simpson's comment on Wilson's trip in his "Editorial," CMAW 27 (April 6, 1907): 157.

[40] Menzies, *Anointed*, 66. Ironically, it was the same Cook who returned to Indianapolis from Los Angeles in 1915 with the Oneness "revelation."

[41] See both Eldridge's district report in AR (1906–07): 58, which is silent about "tongues," and the report of the Alliance superintendent, C. H. Chrisman, who succeeded Eldridge, in AR (1907–08): 67. On the banning of the meetings and Eldridge's prohibition of Cook's teaching, see "George N. Eldridge," AG *Heritage* 5 (Winter 1985–86): 15; Alice Reynolds Flower, "When Pentecost Came to Indianapolis," AG *Heritage* 5 (Winter 1985–86): 5–6; cf. J. Roswell Flower, "The Present Position of Pentecost," PE (June 13, 1925): 7, regarding the explosive effects of Cook's visit.

[42] See Simpson's entry for June 1907 in his ND, 1. For a Pentecostal version of events, see Flower, "When Pentecost Came to Indianapolis," 5–6.

[43] See the entry for May 1909, in ND, 1.

[44] The conventions were held at Indianapolis (June 15–23); Toronto (June 23–July 1); Tulley Lake, N.Y. (July 6–14); Rocky Springs, Lancaster, Penn. (July 12–21); Nyack, N.Y. (July 6–14); Old Orchard Beach, Me. (August 2–12); Beulah Park, Cleveland, Ohio (August 9–18); and Chicago (August 29–September 1). For instances of tongues at the conventions, see Simpson's editorials in CMAW 28 (July 6, 1907): 313; CMAW 28 (July 27, 1907): 37; CMAW 28 (August 17, 1907): 73; cf. "Notes from the

William T. MacArthur, Mr. and Mrs. Daniel W. Kerr, and David McDowell.[45] The spiritual intensity of the 1907 summer conventions was evident to those in attendance. Simpson favorably evaluated them as uniquely blessed by

> a season of quiet, but deep spiritual blessing; prolonged altar services, some lasting 'til the break of day, the dedication of young lives to foreign service, an unusual measure of various gifts and graces; some of the largest congregations and offerings for missionary work.[46]

He singled out the Beulah Park, Ohio, convention as a "Pentecostal convention," the "greatest" and "most marvelous" of its kind in Alliance history. The outpouring of the Spirit there took the form of tongues speaking, healings, exorcisms, confession, intercessory prayer, and extraordinarily generous offerings.[47]

The charismatic momentum of the summer conventions continued unabated into the fall. In October, at Simpson's Gospel Tabernacle in New York, the annual convention was the scene of more "signs and wonders" and all-night tarrying meetings. According to David McDowell, one young lady reportedly sang a "heavenly" melody in tongues and was suspended five or six feet in the air.[48] Harold Moss, later principal of the Beulah Heights Bible and Missionary Training School, was present that night during the convention and described the most unusual scene:

> people were slain everywhere under the mighty power of God, including the ministers on the platform. The case of one young lady, Miss Grace Hanmore (who since has become my wife), was quite remarkable. She was caught away in the Spirit and rendered wholly oblivious to anything natural. A sweet spirit of holy song came forth in notes like that of a nightingale and it

Home Field," CMAW 28 (September 7, 1907): 116; "Notes from the Home Field," CMAW 28 (September 14, 1907): 128.

[45]For accounts of the experiences of these persons during the summer conventions of 1907, see Frodsham, Signs, 46–50.

[46]Simpson: "Editorial," CMAW 28 (August 17, 1907): 73; "Old Orchard Convention," CMAW 28 (August 17, 1907): 106.

[47]Simpson, "Beulah Park Convention," CMAW 28 (September 14, 1907): 128. See W. A. Cramer's report that the Beulah Park Convention in 1908 continued to be a thriving Alliance center of Pentecostal and "latter rain" teaching. Though there was "divergency of views" (but not "confusion"), the "seeking" meetings were continuous ("Notes from the Home Field," CMAW 30 [September 12, 1908]: 402–3).

[48]As quoted in Frodsham, Signs, 51.

filled the whole building. The power of God took hold of the physical and she was raised bodily from the floor three distinct times. She afterwards stated she had seen a vision of a golden ladder and had started to climb it.[49]

He further claimed that these events were "authenticated" by Simpson.[50]

Student life at the Missionary Training Institute was also inundated by utterances in tongues during the months following the summer conventions. The level of spiritual expectation was high, as certain members of the student body were intent upon receiving Spirit baptism with the sign of tongues. In his 1908 report to the Alliance Council, the principal, W. C. Stevens, an advocate of the "latter rain" but wary of fanaticism, confirmed that over the previous school year there had been "much demonstration and in many 'tongues.'"[51] At the same time, he emphasized that the "regular routine" of the school had not been unduly "disturbed" nor had true "spiritual freedom" been compromised by these manifestations.[52] The new effusions of spiritual fervor had been channeled effectively into wholesome activities.[53]

The testimonies of students attending the Institute in 1907 corroborate Stevens's report. Mary Norton, writing over a decade later from India, recalled:

> There had been a revival in the school and there was a kind of hush over the students. Some were definitely seeking the Pentecostal experience, I among them. So we went along until the

---

[49]Ibid., 51–52. Moss's mother, Virginia E. Moss, visited Nyack during the revival of 1907–08, after which she received the Pentecostal baptism with tongues. See Gary B. McGee, "Moss, Virginia E. (1875–1919)," DPCM, 630. Cf. Mary Norton's confirmation of "remarkable manifestations of the Holy Spirit's power" during the October 1907 convention at the Gospel Tabernacle ("The Fullness of the Spirit," TF 38 [January 1918]: 21).

[50]Frodsham, *Signs*, 52.

[51]W. C. Stevens, "Report from the Missionary Institute, Nyack, N.Y.," AR (1907–08), 82. On Stevens's espousal of the "latter rain" theory, see his article "The Latter Rain," LT 7 (September 1907): 521–31, in which he recommended an active seeking of Spirit baptism while avoiding fleshly excesses. "Spiritual intoxication" was to be balanced with a commitment to world evangelization. His article was published again in TF 28 (July 1908): 157–61.

[52]W. C. Stevens, "Report from the Missionary Institute, Nyack, N.Y.," AR (1907–08): 82.

[53]Ibid.

closing night of the school. Some were in prayer in the Chapel all of the memorable night. . . .

At daylight the next morning one of the girls came to my room and said, "Get up and come down to the Chapel. One of the girls is speaking in tongues." I hurried down and found . . . one of the younger girls. . . . She was facing a map of Africa, and was pointing at it and talking in tongues.[54]

Norton's own Spirit baptism with tongues happened toward the end of the year.[55] Similar experiences of tongues speaking among Nyack students continued as late as 1909, after the peak of the Pentecostal controversy in the Alliance had passed.[56]

During 1907, manifestations of spiritual gifts associated with the "latter rain" occurred not only in American Alliance settings but also on overseas mission fields where missionaries had already established a stable presence. The fact that some of the overseas Alliance workers who attended the May 1907 council in Nyack had earlier experienced a Spirit baptism with tongues, which they subsequently desired for their co-workers, no doubt contributed to the hunger "for a special manifestation of the presence and power of the Holy Spirit" that Simpson observed among many of the delegates.[57] Listening to his returning missionaries' reports of their experiences, Simpson was persuaded

---

[54]Norton, "Fullness of the Spirit," 21; cf. Alice Frodsham's account of students seeking Spirit baptism and receiving it with tongues in Stanley H. Frodsham, *Jesus Is Victor. A Story of Grace, Gladness and Glory in the Life of Alice Mary Frodsham* (Springfield, Mo.: Gospel Publishing House, 1930), 36–40.

[55]Norton, "Fullness of the Spirit," 22.

[56]See the report of the Norwegian student, Agnes N. T. Beckdahl, *A Witness of God's Faithfulness* (Lucknow, India: Lucknow Publishing House, n.d.), 37, 38. Cf. the account of Wycliffe and Mary Smith, *Historical Sketches of the Minneapolis Gospel Tabernacle* (Minneapolis: by the church, ca. 1930) (no pagination), who testify to having been "brought . . . into the truth of the Baptism of the Holy Spirit according to Acts 2:4" while studying at Nyack during 1920–21. They received tongues in 1922 in Minneapolis. For an extended discussion of Pentecostal activities at Nyack, see Gary B. McGee, "Pentecostal Awakenings at Nyack," *Paraclete* 18 (Summer 1984): 22–28.

[57]See Simpson, "Editorial," CMAW 27 (June 8, 1907): 205. David McDowell reported that many Alliance workers who came to the council from various parts of the world were already accustomed to speaking in tongues. As quoted in Frodsham, *Signs*, rev. ed., 47; cf. the entry for June 1, 1907, in the diary of Alice Wood (veteran Alliance missionary) regarding the "seeking" meetings that accompanied the council in which some persons received tongues. Her diary is in the AG Archives in Springfield, Mo.

that the "latter rain" was indeed falling on Alliance mission fields and that it was being accompanied by "undoubtedly well authenticated instances of the 'gift of tongues.' "[58]

As early as 1906, missionaries at the Gujarat Station in India were involved in an indigenous revival, which Simpson reported as "spontaneous and profound."[59] It featured a "remarkable movement . . . of Divine healing" that inhibited local diseases, as well as "in many cases" guiding persons into "a deeper religious experience accompanied by the baptism of the Holy Spirit."[60] The official North American Alliance version of the Indian revival, while highlighting the instances of divine healing, was silent regarding any occurrence of tongues. As early as November 1906, however, The Apostolic Faith, a Pentecostal magazine published by the leadership at Azusa Street, identified tongues, prophecy, dreams and visions, the discernment of spirits, and the prayer of faith as having a place in the awakening.[61] The later independent accounts of Alliance missionaries confirmed their experiences of Spirit baptism with tongues.[62] Similar reports in the official Indian Alliance publication during 1908 disclosed the presence of tongues and other charismatic manifestations as characteristic of the revival.[63]

---

[58]Simpson, "Editorial," CMAW 27 (June 8, 1907): 205.

[59]See the summary account of the Indian revival of 1906 in "Annual Report of the President and General Superintendent of the Christian and Missionary Alliance," in AR (1906–07): 11–12, esp. 11; and Ekvall, Fifty Years, 135. More recently see the first Indian Alliance edition of Helen S. Dyer, Revival in India. A report of the 1905–1906 Revival (Akola, India: Alliance Publications, 1987), 101–11. Dyer's book was first published in 1907 by the Gospel Publishing House in New York.

[60]Simpson, "Annual Report," AR (1906–07): 11–12, 14.

[61]See "Pentecost in India," The Apostolic Faith 1 (November 1906): 1.

[62]The experiences of Spirit baptism with tongues of Alliance missionaries Sarah Coxe, Kate Knight, Laura Gardner, and Christian Schoonmaker are recounted in Frodsham, Signs, 134–36; Frank J. Ewart, The Phenomenon of Pentecost (Houston: Herald, 1947), 68–69; and Violet Schoonmaker, A Man Who Loved the Will of God (Landour, Mussoorie: R. T. Hyratt, Hyratt Press, 1959), 8–13. In 1908, reports of Alliance missionaries in India speaking in tongues appeared in the Alliance magazine. See Kate Knight's testimony in "For His Glory," CMAW 29 (January 25, 1908): 274; and the excerpt from A. C. Snead's letter in "India," CMAW 30 (May 16, 1908): 116.

[63]See the report by Mrs. W. M. Turnbull in the India Alliance 7 (May 1908): 131–32, as quoted in Nerius Peter Dholakia, "A Survey and Critical Evaluation of the Christian and Missionary Alliance Ministries in Gujarat" (M.Th. thesis, South Asia Institute of Advanced Christian Studies, 1990),

In the months following the 1907 council in Nyack, Robert Jaffray, field secretary of the South China Alliance Mission, reported an unprecedented leaderless movement of the Spirit that climaxed in the "quiet" manifestations of tongues among missionaries and natives alike.[64] He disclaimed any outside influence at work in promoting the gift of tongues, claiming instead that it was "an entirely new experience" not out of keeping with other simultaneous outpourings of the "latter rain" around the world.[65] Moreover, Jaffray underlined the need for a "spirit of discernment" so as not to be led astray by extremism from the foremost objective of evangelizing the heathen. The "peculiar and subtle dangers" attached to "outward physical manifestations" did not, however, negate the value of what Jaffray and others had experienced. For Jaffray, when appreciated for what it is, the anointing of the Spirit accompanied by tongues was a "profound blessing" that bore "lasting fruit" and gave added empowerment to the missionary enterprise.[66]

In some instances, such as South China, the new experience of tongues speaking was successfully integrated with the older deeper-life tradition of Alliance spirituality, and schism was averted. Many years later the missionaries in authority in the field were lauded by the British Pentecostal theologian and historian Donald Gee for their sagacious response to the "Pentecostal Revival," atypical of the "fear and prejudice" more often encountered by the movement in its early years.[67] Other fields, however, underwent much stress and strain as a result of "latter rain" inspired Spirit baptisms marked by tongues. Alliance works in India, China and Tibet (other than South China), Egypt, the West Indies, Africa, Persia, Mongolia, and Latin America all suffered the loss of missionaries who chose to leave and align themselves with the Pentecostal movement.[68]

86–87; cf. further accounts of tongues-speaking in the *India Alliance* 8 (September 1908): 26; *India Alliance* 8 (December 1908): 64.

[64]See Jaffray's report in "South China," AR (1907–08): 7, 142–43, esp. 143; cf. Simpson's summary of events in South China in which he commended Jaffray and others for their proper managing of the "crisis" ("Annual Report of the President and General Superintendent of the Christian and Missionary Alliance," AR [1907–08]: 41–42).

[65]Jaffray, "South China," AR (1907–08): 143.

[66]Ibid.

[67]Gee, *Wind and Flame*, 44.

[68]See the list of departing Alliance missionaries, and other per-

Simpson's Critique of the Pentecostal Movement

Simpson's criticisms of the Pentecostal movement cen-
tered on the doctrine of tongues as the "initial evidence" of Spirit
baptism, a teaching that he regarded as an offense to sound
biblical doctrine and injurious to unity. He charged that Pentecostals, in promoting the "initial evidence" doctrine, had fallen
prey to one of the "evils of the apostolic age" against which Paul
had written.[69] Furthermore, he reasoned that the biblically unwar-
ranted exaltation of tongues was responsible for the metamor-
phosis of what had begun as a "genuine movement of the Holy
Spirit" into a movement fraught with "extravagance," "excess,"
"serious error," "wildfire," and "fanaticism."[70] When compared with
the ecumenical, tolerant flavor of the Alliance, Pentecostal
preaching on the "evidence doctrine" was a flagrant violation of
Christian unity and displayed a "narrow" and "uncharitable" attitude toward other Christians.[71]

Pentecostal insistence on the inseparability of Spirit
baptism and tongues indirectly created a dialectic in Simpson's
theology of Spirit baptism, holiness, and supernatural gifts.
Confronted by an ostensible Pentecostal overemphasis on manifestations of the Spirit, Simpson at times seemed to deemphasize
the baptism of the Holy Spirit as a source of power for service.
Instead he accentuated its role in bringing "union with Christ,
cleansing from sin and equipment for [one's] practical Christian
life."[72] In an editorial in September 1906, he wrote:

> It [the baptism of the Holy Spirit] is not merely a baptism of
> power; power is merely incidental to it. It is the baptism with
> the Holy Ghost[,] and His coming brings holiness, happiness,
> healing and all the fullness of God.[73]

Since gifts of the Spirit do not have a bearing on one's conversion
and growth in holiness, it amounted to a "pernicious error" to

---

sonnel who later became Pentecostal missionaries, constructed by McGee
in *This Gospel*, 1:62–63.

[69]Simpson, "Editorial," CMAW 26 (November 17, 1906): 305.

[70]Simpson, "Annual Report," AR (1906–07): 5; cf. Simpson: "Editorial," CMAW 27 (February 2, 1907): 49; "Fervor and Fanaticism," CMAW 26
(December 22, 1906): 391.

[71]Simpson, "Editorial," AW 37 (January 27, 1912): 258.

[72]Simpson, "Editorial," CMAW 29 (October 19, 1907): 38.

[73]Simpson, "Editorial," LT 6 (September 1906): 513.

make the presence of spiritual gifts a necessary indicator of having received the Holy Spirit.[74] Disturbed by Pentecostalism's seeming obsession with certain supernatural gifts, Simpson appeared to temper his earlier restorationist yearnings for spiritual manifestations to the point where he deemed it more constructive to recommend the "practical and useful" benefits of love over the "sensational" gifts of power.[75]

During 1907 and 1908 when the Pentecostal crisis was at its highest, Simpson's publications were liberally seasoned with anti-Pentecostal articles by his associates and others. Each had the same intent: to refute the initial evidence doctrine and to curb aberrations in the realm of spiritual gifts.[76] In 1907, Simpson's article "Gifts and Grace," which was also published in the *Alliance Weekly*, preached as a sermon, and distributed in tract form, appeared in a collection of essays entitled *The Signs of the Times*.[77] As in the past, Simpson affirmed the value of all spiritual gifts, including tongues, when their use is governed by self-control, love, and respect for order. These principles were to be upheld even at the risk of being misrepresented as "quenching the Spirit."[78] The allusions to Pentecostal excesses, however, were unmistakable. Clairvoyance and spiritualism lurked on the fringes of a pre-

---

[74]Simpson, "Gifts and Grace," 302; cf. the meditation for the twenty-fourth day in Simpson, *Comforter*, where he describes the doctrine as "extreme" and "most unscriptural."

[75]See the meditation for the twenty-fourth day in Simpson, *Comforter*. In his article "Spiritual Sanity," LT 7 (April 1907): 194, he argues for the inferiority of tongues to other more useful gifts.

[76]For example, see "True and False Fire," LT 7 (January 1907): 40–46; J. Hudson Ballard, "Spiritual Gifts with Special Reference to the Gift of Tongues," LT 7 (January 1907): 23–31; Joseph Smale, "The Gift of Tongues," LT 7 (January 1907): 32–43; F. W. Farr, "The Baptism of the Holy Spirit," CMAW 29 (October 26, 1907): 55–56; Mary B. Mullen, "Some Danger Lines," CMAW 29 (November 2, 1907): 75; A. J. Ramsey, "The Receiving of the Holy Spirit and the Baptism in the Holy Spirit—Identical or Different?" CMAW 29 (February 22, 1908): 345–46; C. J. Moon, "The Receiving of the Holy Ghost," CMAW 29 (February 22, 1908): 30; A. J. Ramsey, "Speaking with Tongues. An Exegetical Study," CMAW 30 (April 4, 1908): 7–17; May Maybbette Anderson, "Deceptive Leadings," CMAW 30 (April 11, 1908): 25–40; William T. MacArthur, "The Phenomenon of Supernatural Utterance," CMAW 31 (October 31, 1908): 72–73; M. A. Dean, "Some Bible Evidences of the Baptism of the Holy Ghost," CMAW 32 (April 3, 1909): 7–8.

[77]Philip Mauro et al., *The Signs of the Times or God's Message for Today*, 95–113.

[78]Ibid., 110.

occupation with tongues.[79] The initial evidence doctrine was denounced as "rash and wholly unscriptural" and guilty of exalting a "mere manifestation of the Holy Ghost" above the Spirit's "higher ministry of grace."[80] The Pentecostal movement itself was in danger of being overrun by "unwise and reckless leaders" and populated by persons of "doubtful character or spiritual qualifications."[81] Nevertheless, in the heat of the furor, he exhorted his followers

> not [to] fear or ignore any of the gifts and manifestations of the Holy Ghost, no matter how extraordinary; but [to] be prepared to expect God to reveal Himself to His people, especially in these last days, in many signal and glorious ways.[82]

Simpson's report to the 1907 Alliance Council concluded that the preceding year (1906) had been "a year of the Holy Spirit" that had brought renewal to every facet of the work. In many instances the manifestations of tongues accompanying this visitation did not detract from the "genuine marks of the presence of 'the Spirit of power, love and a sound mind.' " On other occasions, however, tongues speaking was discredited by "extravagance, excess and serious error." These situations were exacerbated by persons insisting that tongues was the "essential evidence" of Spirit baptism. Simpson cautioned the council not to let "the counterfeit" usurp the place of "the genuine gold."[83]

Following the conclusion of the 1907 council, Simpson's assessment of Pentecostalism was ambivalent. In a June 1907 editorial appearing in his publication *Living Truths*, he wrote:

> In several places the movement appears to have been genuine and fruitful only of good. In other places it seems to have resulted in division, extravagance and fanaticism, and to have

---

[79]Ibid., 104–5.

[80]Ibid., 110.

[81]Ibid., 109.

[82]Ibid. For Simpson's efforts to counter the Pentecostal insistence on supernatural gifts by advancing his own concept of the nature and use of spiritual power, see his several articles on the subject in the second half of 1907: "The Exceeding Greatness of His Power," CMAW 28 (July 6, 1907): 314–15; "The Wonder-Working God," CMAW 29 (October 19, 1907): 41–42; and "The Holy Spirit and Missions," CMAW 29 (October 26, 1907): 57–58.

[83]Simpson, "Annual Report," AR (1906–07): 5.

fallen into the hands of persons of doubtful reputation and ill-balanced mind.[84]

A year later, despite the alleged errors of Pentecostals, Simpson still did not say that the movement as a whole warranted condemnation. Where it was guided by strong and wise leadership, it bore impressive spiritual fruit that could not be disputed.[85] He aligned himself with the "Gamaliel" position taken by a conference of German pastors convoked at Barmen in December 1907, called not to "promote or oppose the movement" but to wait on God for a further discernment of truth.[86] In his presidential report on "Special Revival Movements," given to the 1908 Alliance Council, however, he enumerated the negative effects of Pentecostalism. The "evidence doctrine" had misled some people to seek special manifestations rather than God, with the by-product of reduced evangelistic concern. He accused those who laid claim to Spirit baptism with tongues of lighting sectarian fires that consumed Alliance branches and diminished the flow of missionary contributions. Some inexperienced persons had been commissioned to foreign countries under the naive assumption that they would receive the gift of tongues as a substitute for language study, only to be disappointed and abandoned. Lastly, Simpson pinpointed the prevalence of a "prophetic authority" within the movement which smacked of "the Romish confessional" or "spiritualism."[87] He finished his report by contrasting this portrait of Pentecostal deviance to the superior example of the Alliance, which modeled spiritual freedom in a controlled atmosphere respectful of biblical priorities.[88]

The overall tone of the report reflected the duress of the previous year. Prior to the 1908 council, the Alliance founder had reviewed 1907 as a year when stability had been jeopardized and

---

[84]Simpson, "The Gift of Tongues," LT 7 (June 1907): 312.

[85]Simpson, "Annual Report," AR (1907–08): 10.

[86]Simpson, "Editorial," CMAW 29 (February 29, 1908): 366. He also expressed his agreement with the German pastor Stockmayer's opposition to the "initial evidence" doctrine, publicized while visiting New York City in 1909. See his "Editorial," CMAW 30 (February 27, 1909): 364. Stockmayer was a prominent participant in the international healing and holiness movement with which Simpson was associated. For a report of his view on tongues, see Simpson, "Pastor O. Stockmayer on the Gift of Tongues," CMAW 31 (March 13, 1909): 397.

[87]Simpson: "Annual Report," AR (1907–08): 11, 12.

[88]Ibid., 13.

a revival climate that had been growing since 1905 had turned somewhat sour because of extremism. In an April 1908 editorial, he capsulated developments to date:

> One year ago [1907] our hearts were bowed in deep and over-whelming prayer that God would guide the little ship of our Alliance work through the cross currents, the shifting tides and the contrary winds which were beginning to seek us around in every direction. It has been a year of stress and strain. Along with much that was holy and divine, there have also been the wild waves of fanaticism and the bitter strife of tongues leading to division and almost dismemberment of some branches of the work.[89]

By 1908, he assumed the worst of the crisis to have passed, alleging for the most part that it had been weathered and that the Alliance was still intact:

> the spirit of wisdom and love has prevailed and we have reports of profound spiritual awakenings and a loyal and divided devotion to our common trust and especially the great work of the world's evangelization. We believe . . . that there is room within our simple organization for all the heights and depths of the Holy Spirit's grace and power along with the simple and practical trust which has been committed to our hands in the Fourfold Gospel.[90]

Simpson prized, above all, the unity of the Alliance, founded on a "common experience" and "precious revelation" of Jesus as "Savior, Sanctifier, Healer, and Coming Lord," and on a common commitment to the task of world evangelization. The preservation

---

[89]Simpson, "Editorial," CMAW 30 (April 4, 1908): 10.

[90]Ibid. A survey of the number of references to tongues speaking and Pentecostalism in Simpson's magazines may give some indication of the rise and decline of Pentecostal influence upon the Alliance. The number of references is as follows:

Year	Number of References
1905 —	13
1906 —	15
1907 —	34 (peak year)
1908 —	10
1909 —	9

This research has been done by Alliance historian John Sawin, "Response and Attitude," 47.

of unity was vital to the ongoing success of the Alliance. It could remain only as long as Alliance workers, given their diverse denominational backgrounds, could see Christ in one another.[91] The internal disagreements over the "latter rain" and Spirit baptism were not to be resolved by any ecclesiastical authority. Simpson and the Alliance Board of Managers considered them matters of personal conviction and liberty. They viewed any attempts to legislate doctrine in these areas, beyond simply affirming the Fourfold Gospel, as likely to bring more bondage than freedom.[92]

The Pentecostal initial evidence doctrine tore at the Fourfold fabric of Alliance unity. When some of Pentecostal persuasion desired to establish a new organization, Simpson countered that there was no need for this since the Alliance embraced "all the Scriptural manifestations of the Holy Ghost."[93] While those who legitimized schism had invariably come to esteem themselves as "more highly gifted spiritually than others," Simpson articulated a less positive perspective on their actions.[94] He accused certain of those pursuing a "special" Spirit baptism of "smallness . . . meanness . . . gossiping, criticizing, back-biting, slandering and condemning other Christians."[95] They were responsible for luring supporters away from branch meetings and regular services to participate in "partisan movements and meetings."[96] Such factious Pentecostal gatherings were deplored by Simpson as inimical to the Alliance cause.[97]

It was mostly Simpson's pastoral concerns that gave rise to his fear that abuses of spiritual gifts would undermine the effort to sustain an atmosphere of true spiritual liberty. Invariably, many, in his estimation, sought Spirit baptism with tongues only because they felt they were not truly baptized until they had it. More regrettably, the excessively indulgent behavior of some

---

[91] Simpson, "Editorial," CMAW 30 (August 1, 1908): 296.

[92] Simpson, "Editorial," CMAW 29 (March 28, 1908): 432; cf. the "Resolution of the Board of the C.&M.A., Saturday, March 21, 1908, Regarding the 'Latter Rain Movement,' " AR (1907–08): 13.

[93] Simpson, "Editorial," CMAW 28 (July 6, 1907): 313.

[94] Simpson, "Editorial," CMAW 28 (July 13, 1907): 13.

[95] Simpson, "Editorial," CMAW 30 (September 26, 1908): 430.

[96] Simpson, "Editorial," CMAW 30 (September 19, 1908): 414.

[97] Regarding the depletion of funds for Alliance missionary concerns caused by defections, see Simpson's editorials in CMAW 30 (April 4, 1908): 10; AW 40 (September 6, 1913): 353.

in their exercise of spiritual gifts became "scarecrows" to sincere Christians whose fear of "certain manifestations" inhibited them from seeking the real blessing of God.[98] The stakes were high. If discernment and sanity were not present in the church, then "rational Christians" would "be turned away" from the genuine manifestations of divine power out of fear of the counterfeit.[99] One could expect that "delusions and counterfeits," if left undiscerned, would follow closely on the heels of genuine revival and dissipate it.[100] Simpson reminded his readers that in the restoration of divine healing during the previous century, the devil had tried to thwart the recovery of apostolic truth by raising up Spiritualism and Christian Science as imitations. Thus he cautioned his workers to be on guard against the activities of the same diabolical forces of deception present in the Pentecostal movement.[101]

As a strategy of preventing further encroachments on their constituency, Alliance authorities endeavored to tighten the lines of supervision. Simpson directed those branches desiring "special services and larger blessing" to consult with a state or district superintendent in order to obtain a "wise evangelist or authorized leader." He advised against gravitating to the "unknown and . . . unwise [Pentecostal] shepherds" who would exploit sincere spiritual seekers for their own gain and thereby inflict greater losses on the Alliance.[102] Trying to offset the attraction of "men or women who seem to have supernatural gifts and powers," Simpson counseled his troops to look to those individuals whose ministries were accredited on the basis of their "long-suffering love," not their "power, light or mystery."[103] As an additional protective measure, the Alliance eventually adopted a "reversion clause" in its new constitution at the 1912 Council in Boone, Iowa. This legislative innovation guaranteed that the property of local branches, schools, and nondenominational

---

[98]Simpson, "Side Issues and the Supreme Object of Life," CMAW 30 (September 19, 1908): 416.

[99]Simpson, "Editorial," CMAW 31 (January 23, 1909): 280.

[100] Simpson, "Spiritual Sanity," LT 7 (April 1907): 191.

[101] On the need for caution and discernment in assessing spiritual phenomena, see ibid., 191, 194, and Simpson's editorials in CMAW 25 (March 1906): 185; CMAW 26 (November 17, 1906): 305; CMAW 29 (October 19, 1907): 38.

[102] Simpson, "Editorial," CMAW 29 (October 19, 1907): 37.

[103] Simpson, "Editorial," CMAW 30 (April 4, 1908): 10.

churches would revert to the parent society should the property cease to be used as initially intended.[104]

Simpson's evaluation of Pentecostalism as a mixed bless-ing, possessing both the supernatural signs of authentic revival and destructive extremist elements, translated into the pursuit of a policy of moderation. In the midst of heated controversy, he continued to sanction the exercising of spiritual gifts. For him, the problem created by excesses could not be solved by suppress-ing all spiritual manifestations. To the contrary, he asserted that "the only way to meet error [is] to go all the way with truth."[105]

Pentecostal Perceptions of Simpson and the Alliance

Simpson's policy of moderation, which simultaneously accepted the doctrine of the "latter rain" with its implication for the restoration of spiritual gifts, opposed the Pentecostal initial evidence doctrine, and underscored the need for discernment and restraint where supernatural manifestations were "restored," was invariably distorted by certain Pentecostal critics. They were in-clined to see him as negatively disposed to the Pentecostal baptism of the Holy Spirit particularly because of his unyielding stance against the evidence doctrine. One such person was Frank Bartleman, an itinerant evangelist and ambassador of the events he had witnessed at Azusa Street, who zealously propagated Pentecostalism in Alliance circles during his trips to the eastern United States in 1907 and 1908.[106]

The response of Alliance leaders to his ministry was divided. In the Ohio district where W. A. Cramer and Claude A. McKinney had been among the first to receive Spirit baptism with tongues, Bartleman was for the most part received warmly, though he castigated one Ohio Alliance leader as an instrument of the devil for obstructing those seeking the "baptism."[107] Fur-

---

[104] "Constitution and Principles of the Christian and Missionary Alliance," AR (1911–12): 39–50, esp. 49.

[105] Simpson: "Editorial," CMAW 27 (May 4, 1907): 205; "Editorial," CMAW 32 (June 12, 1909): 180.

[106] These trips are described in detail in Frank Bartleman, *How Pentecost Came to Los Angeles. As It Was in the Beginning*, 2d ed. (Los Angeles: published privately, 1925), 97–133. The entire text of the book is in *Witness to Pentecost: The Life of Frank Bartleman*, ed. Donald W. Dayton (New York and London: Garland, 1985).

[107] Ibid., 103–4.

ther east he spoke at the convention in Nyack in July 1907, where he "had not been invited."[108] While in New York City, he visited the Alliance's Stephen Merritt, who was renowned for his pneumatological insights.[109]

Bartleman continued on the Alliance circuit to the annual convention at Old Orchard, Maine, which convened the next month. There he was persona non grata. By his account, he conducted unofficial tarrying meetings in a nearby woods and the village church to accommodate those seeking Spirit baptism with tongues. Apart from one unsanctioned "surprise" appearance on the Old Orchard platform, Bartleman was denied any public exposure.[110] He related his version of the stiff opposition he encountered from the convention authorities:

> A score of hungry souls repaired to the village church for a whole night of prayer, having secured the key from the local pastor. We were not allowed to tarry on the camp grounds. One member of the Nyack C.M.A. faculty got the "baptism" that night. . . . I spoke to this little company in the church . . . as they would allow no meetings of this kind in the camp. The camp meeting committee then forced the pastor to close the church against us. They did not want their people to get the "baptism." We went to the woods again. . . . The committee had no jurisdiction over the woods outside the camp.[111]

To defuse the mounting tension, the off-limits meetings, which attracted as many as one hundred persons, were voluntarily disbanded. What to Bartleman was a mighty blessing of God was to the convention authorities a thorn in the side. He later recalled his precipitous exit from the scene:

> The Lord had blessed so mightily in our little meetings that the camp became stirred. Rather than have further, outbroken trouble, the saints thought it best to discontinue the meetings, and I dropped quietly out of camp before the committee could take any definite further action in the matter. Thus we avoided further unpleasantness and strife. The hungry ones were fairly dogging my steps and thronging me. The committee became afraid of my influence with the people.[112]

---

108 Ibid., 105.
109 Ibid.
110 Ibid., 106.
111 Ibid., 106–7.
112 Ibid., 107. See the veiled reference by an Alliance reporter to

Bartleman's perception of Simpson as an entrenched opponent of the Pentecostal movement surfaced when he recounted the details of an all-night meeting which transpired at the Gospel Tabernacle in New York during the October 1907 convention. His recollection of events approximated those of McDowell and Moss (cited earlier):

> A young girl came under the power and her spirit was caught up to the throne. She sang a melody, without words, that seemed to come from within the veil, it was so heavenly. It seemed to come from another world. I have never heard its equal before or since.[113]

Bartleman interpreted this event as a divine vindication of the Pentecostal movement—right in the mother church of the Alliance:

> A. B. Simpson was there himself that night and was impressed by it. He had been much opposed to the "Pentecostal" work. Doubtless God gave it as a witness to him.[114]

The rest of what followed that night only served to deepen Bartleman's conviction as to the correctness of his interpretation of events:

> Several were slain under the power. Toward morning the presence of the Lord was wonderful. I went to leave the hall just at daybreak and shook hands with a sister hungry for the "baptism." The Spirit came upon her and I could not turn her loose until she fell at the altar, and came through speaking in "tongues." I shook hands with another hungry sister. . . . The Spirit fell upon her and she received the "baptism" right there on her feet, speaking in "tongues" before I could turn her loose. That was a wonderful night.[115]

For Bartleman, the night climaxed a week during which Alliance persons, attending the annual October convention at the Gospel

---

Bartleman's disruptive influence and exploitation of an all-night prayer meeting during the convention in "Old Orchard Convention," CMAW 28 (August 31, 1907): 106.

[113] Bartleman, *Pentecost*, 103; cf. nn. 48 and 49 above. The report given in Simpson's magazine concurred: "There were some marked manifestations of the presence and power of the Holy Spirit and at the meeting on Thursday night it seemed as if the very gates of heaven were opened for a little while to the ears of mortals" ("Notes from the New York Convention," CMAW 29 [October 19, 1907]: 48).

[114] Bartleman, *Pentecost*, 109.

[115] Ibid.

Tabernacle, were also frequenting his meetings (held at a separate location) on a nightly basis after the convention's services were over. According to Bartleman, they were motivated by "hunger for the 'Pentecostal' message."[116]

By the time Bartleman returned to the east in 1908, again endeavoring to penetrate the heart of the Alliance, the lines were clearly drawn. When invited by a Nyack faculty member of Pentecostal persuasion to address the student body of the Missionary Training Institute, Bartleman claimed that "the opposition [at the school] was great by this time."[117] A confrontation ensued:

> The faculty were caught off their guard. Five minutes later they would have canceled the engagement if God had allowed them to. They subjected me to an attempted severe censorship before I went to the platform, as to what I would preach. It tied me up a little, but the Lord gave victory. I was speaking to the students. And they were a hungry lot.[118]

Permitted to speak again the following morning, Bartleman concluded triumphantly that "God touched their hearts in the end."[119]

The uncomplimentary image projected on Simpson and the Alliance by Pentecostals such as Bartleman was repeatedly met with the reply that the Alliance rejected only the exclusivist doctrine of tongues and not the validity of the experience of Spirit baptism. Simpson countered that the Alliance had always affirmed the legitimacy of all the gifts of the Spirit.[120] To portray the organization in any other light amounted to a "gross misrepresentation."[121] He complained that Pentecostals did a disservice to the "wise and conservative people" of the Alliance by making them out to be opponents of the work of the Holy Spirit.[122] As proof of their misguided allegations, he pointed out to his Pentecostal critics that many workers, at home and abroad, had grown in personal piety and devotion to service within the Alli-

---

[116] Ibid.

[117] Ibid., 125.

[118] Ibid. Cf. the same perspective of Alice Frodsham, a student at the time (and later wife of Stanley H. Frodsham, editor of the *Pentecostal Evangel*), who "always felt that this school was given a great opportunity at this time, but some of the leaders were not fully sympathetic with what God was doing." See Stanley H. Frodsham, *Jesus Is Victor*, 40.

[119] Bartleman, *Pentecost*, 125.

[120] Simpson, "Editorial," CMAW 34 (April 30, 1910): 78.

[121] Simpson, "Editorial," AW 37 (January 27, 1912): 258.

[122] Simpson, "Editorial," CMAW 30 (September 19, 1908): 414.

ance as a fruit of their new "baptism."[123] Ironically, Simpson cited the example of the summer convention at Old Orchard in 1907 as further verification of the freedom to be found. Though the teaching offered there was admittedly "careful and, in some respects, conservative," he maintained that every opportunity had been given for seeking and receiving the fullness of the Holy Spirit with all the accompanying gifts and graces: "No restraint whatever was put upon true seekers after truth and life."[124] Bartleman would hardly have concurred. His account of the same convention was one of harassment by the convention's authorities and "underground" tarrying meetings composed of people who sought a more charismatic religious experience than the official agenda permitted.

Simpson went to even greater lengths to dispel notions that workers who had experienced a Spirit baptism with tongues were pressured to leave. On one occasion, he publicly disclosed the complete correspondence between a missionary, Kay Knight, and the Alliance executive in India. His purpose was to allay Pentecostal suspicion that her resignation was required due to her Pentecostal leanings. He rejoined that this was not the case. Rather, it was related to "questions of missionary polity" and not to her recent Pentecostal experience.[125]

Simpson's numerous public references to the extremist elements in the Pentecostal movement, made mostly for pastoral reasons, undoubtedly lay behind some perceptions of him as essentially unsympathetic to those dimensions of apostolic truth that God was supposedly restoring to the church through Pentecostalism. In actuality, however, Simpson's posture toward the movement was more complex than that. What his critics were unable to see was that as a high profile leader he spoke loudest on Pentecostal shortcomings, while at the personal level, the movement, for all its flaws, was inspiring him to take yet another step in his spiritual pilgrimage.

---

[123] Ibid. Cf. his "Editorial," AW 40 (September 6, 1913): 353.

[124] Simpson, "Editorial," CMAW 28 (August 17, 1907): 73.

[125] Simpson, "Retirement of Miss Kate Knight," CMAW 31 (January 30, 1909): 291; cf. idem, "Editorial," CMAW 31 (January 30, 1909): 296. Kate Knight's testimony of her Spirit baptism with tongues had appeared in "For His Glory," CMAW 29 (January 25, 1908): 274. The following month Simpson refuted a religious magazine's claim that Knight's "American mission had cast [her] out" ("Editorial," CMAW 31 [February 20, 1909]: 348). She later acknowledged her "mistake," asked, and was received back into the Alliance. See Simpson, "Editorial," CMAW 31 (March 27, 1909): 432.

SIMPSON AND HIS FOLLOWERS: PERSONAL CHOICES

THE PORTRAIT OF PENTECOSTALISM that Simpson painted in his books, articles, editorials, sermons, and annual presidential reports to the Alliance Council was intended for public consumption. As leader, his primary concerns during the years of the controversy were to protect doctrinal and spiritual unity, sustain the missionary momentum that had been steadily rising since the organization's birth, and halt the flow of persons (and property) who had received Spirit baptism with tongues into the Pentecostal movement. In the light of these objectives, even though he refrained from a categorical condemnation of the movement, his official statements tended to lean in a negative direction, focusing more on Pentecostal flaws than strengths.

At the same time, Simpson was alert to the ultraconservative elements in his constituency who stereotyped the movement by its worst extremes and refused to accept it in any way as a fulfillment of "latter rain" expectations. An editorial he wrote in 1908 seemed to have these persons in mind. He implored them not to use Pentecostal excesses as a pretext for curtailing the desire for a supernatural visitation of the Holy Spirit. Contrarily, Simpson advised that the best way to deter persons who either had already received or were seeking such a visitation from leaving the Alliance and joining the Pentecostals was

to seek and claim such an outpouring of the Holy Spirit in our
[the Alliance's] regular work that God will be able to vindicate
His own cause by His presence and power in our midst,—that
no true heart can find any pretext for going elsewhere for
spiritual food and reviving fire.[1]

Simpson took his own counsel to heart.

Simpson as "Seeker"

To determine accurately Simpson's complete response to
Pentecostalism requires the historian to come to grips with both
the public concerns of Simpson, the conscientious leader of an
interdenominational organization still in a process of consolidation, and his personal aspirations as spiritual pilgrim whose life
had been receptive to and altered by "new truths" to which he had
been exposed by various movements in the nineteenth century. A
personal diary covering the period from 1907 to 1916, neglected
until very recently, reveals in an intimate way the intensification
of Simpson's spiritual longings in the midst of the turmoil of the
Pentecostal controversy.[2]

Prior to the crucial May 1907 Alliance Council at Nyack,
Simpson, with the prophet Daniel as his inspiration, was led to
enter a time of prayer and fasting to receive a "special anointing
of the Holy Ghost." He was motivated both by his concern for the
approaching council and by his desire for discernment regarding
his personal relationship to and role in what he saw as a concurrent "special movement of the Holy Spirit abroad."[3] This period of
"waiting on God" consumed the three weeks prior to the council.[4]

---

[1] Simpson, "Editorial," CMAW 30 (September 19, 1908): 414.

[2] Only a typed copy of the diary is extant. It can be found in the
Canadian Bible College/Canadian Theological Seminary Archives in Re-
gina, Saskatchewan. It was first given attention by Alliance historians in
John Sawin, "The Response and Attitude of Dr. A. B. Simpson and The
Christian and Missionary Alliance to the Tongues Movement of 1906–1920"
(Paper delivered at the Society for Pentecostal Studies, Costa Mesa, Calif.,
15 November 1986), 18–21, 28; Robert Niklaus et al., All for Jesus. God at Work
in the Christian and Missionary Alliance Over One Hundred Years (Camp Hill,
Penn.: Christian Publications: 1986), 113–14; and Charles Nienkirchen,
"A. B. Simpson: Forerunner and Critic of the Pentecostal Movement," in
Birth of a Vision, 148–49.

[3] See entry for May 1907, in ND, 1.

[4] Ibid.

As a result, he was receptive to and discerning of all that transpired at the council. The occurrences of tongues and "other extraordinary manifestations" were judged by Simpson both as "genuine" and as characterized by unedifying, individual "eccentricities." This caused him to reaffirm "quietly" his longstanding conviction about the need for spiritual gifts to be expressed publicly in accordance with the apostolic guidelines laid out in 1 Corinthians 12 and 14. His posture was one of guarded openness to charismatic manifestations. The diary indicates: "[He] could not question the reality of the gifts, and . . . was led to pray much about it, and for God's highest will and glory in connection with it."[5]

When Simpson came to the Indianapolis convention the following month (June), he was apprehensive, given the split over tarrying meetings and tongues that had occurred there previously. Nevertheless, his expectation remained high that "nothing less than [the Spirit's] perfect and mighty fullness might come into [his] life."[6] At the Nyack convention in July 1907, Simpson recorded an electrifying moment in his search for a renewal of unction:

> On the closing Saturday of the Nyack Convention I received, as I waited in the aftermeeting, a distinct touch of the mighty power of the Holy Spirit—a kind of breaking through accompanied by a sense of awe and a lighting up of my senses. It was as if a wedge of light and power were being driven through my inmost being and I all broken open [sic]. I welcomed it.[7]

Disappointed that the meeting was "abruptly closed" by the person in charge, Simpson remained conscious of a "peculiar power" and "a sort of 'weight of love' " that rested on him throughout the ensuing days.[8]

In August 1907, Simpson was present at Old Orchard, Maine, which was "holy ground" to him. Contemplating his past spiritual journey, he renewed his "covenant of healing" (as he did annually) in the same wooded spot where he had first experienced divine healing in 1881.[9] This time, however, the need for a new baptism of the Holy Spirit was preeminent in his mind:

---

[5] Ibid.
[6] Ibid., entry for June 1907.
[7] Ibid., entry for July 28, 1907.
[8] Ibid.
[9] Ibid., entry for August 9, 1907.

I pressed upon Him a new claim for a Mighty Baptism of the Holy Ghost in His complete Pentecostal fullness embracing all the gifts and graces of the Spirit for my special need at this time and for the new conditions and needs of my life and work. He met me as I lay upon my face before Him with a distinct illumination, and then as the Presence began to fade and I cried out to Him to stay. He bade me *believe* [his emphasis] and take it all by simple faith as I had taken my healing 26 years before. I did so, and was enabled definitely to believe and claim in all and rest in Him.[10]

Not disparaging the Spirit baptism that had launched his "higher life" in Louisville over thirty years before, Simpson was now seeking for a "deeper and fuller baptism." He received fresh divine assurances of the appropriateness of his quest through Isaiah 49:8 and Acts 1:8.[11] No longer content with his habitual practice of contemplative prayer, Simpson "felt there was *more*" (his emphasis) and looked forward to a "most wonderful manifestation of His presence," the scope of which would exceed any kind of Spirit baptism hitherto experienced.[12]

Returning to Nyack in late August after the Beulah Park, Ohio, convention, Simpson's seeking continued unabated. At home sitting on his lawn, he

had a special season of mighty prayer, in which God revealed to [him] the NAME of JESUS in special power and enabled [him] to plead it within the veil for an hour or more until it seemed to bear [sic] down every barrier and to command all that [he] could ask. He also let [him] plead at great length Jeremiah 33:3 in the fullness of its meaning as God saw it, and to ask for "great and mighty things which [he] KNEW NOT."[13]

Despite an "utterly new revelation of [Christ's] power and glory," Simpson sensed that there was yet "*much more*" (his emphasis) for him which exceeded his previous twenty-six years of experience in the Fourfold Gospel.[14] A few days later he recorded another divine visitation: "a very mighty and continued resting of the Spirit [came] down upon my body until it was almost over-

---

[10]Ibid.
[11]Ibid., 2.
[12]Ibid.
[13]Ibid., entry for August 22, 1907.
[14]Ibid.

powering and continued during much of the night."[15] By this time, Simpson was prepared to relinquish all timidity in the matter of spiritual gifts and to "fully take all that is promised in HIS NAME" (his emphasis).[16]

In September 1907, following what he termed "remark-able seasons of prayer, fellowship and blessing," Simpson re-sumed his liturgy of prayer and fasting in his persistent search for the blessing he coveted.[17] His daily practice of spiritual dis-ciplines was reinforced by times of solitude and night sessions of prayer.[18] On the occasion of a trip to Hamilton, Ontario, to com-memorate the forty-second anniversary of his ordination, Simp-son was drawn to the Pentecostal promise in Joel 2:26–28 in anticipation of being "ordain[ed] . . . anew."[19] Fittingly, on the anniversary day, "the Spirit came with a baptism of Holy laughter for an hour or more," though even this coming of the Spirit did not satiate his inner thirst.[20] The next day, Simpson was im-mersed for six hours in "a distinct sense of . . . warmth . . . a penetrating fire," which at first he mistook for a "fever" but which he later interpreted symbolically as the commencement of a second ordination with "new power."[21]

Despite the unique sense of the divine presence to which Simpson testified during August and September 1907, the diary indicates that his personal expectations were not fully met. He had certainly undergone a crescendo of spiritual awakening but

> at the same time there was a deep sense of much more to come and that [his] heart could not be satisfied without all the fullness of His power. The prayer went up spontaneously for all His fullness and power and the promise repeated itself over and over again. "Ask in my Name . . . that your joy may be full."[22]

After a five-year hiatus in the diary, an entry for October 6, 1912, removes the innuendo and clarifies precisely the object of Simp-son's quest—Spirit baptism with tongues. The Scriptures, the need of personal renewal, and the testimonies of close friends

---

[15]Ibid., entry for August 28, 1907.
[16]Ibid.
[17]Ibid., entry for September 5, 1907.
[18]Ibid., entries for September 6, 12, 13, 14, 1907, 3, 4.
[19]Ibid., entry for September 10, 1907, 3.
[20]Ibid., entry for September 12, 1907.
[21]Ibid., entry for September 13, 1907.
[22]Ibid., entry for September 14, 1907, 4.

and numerous Alliance workers prompted Simpson to seek such an experience from 1907 through 1912. At the end of this period, however, he concluded:

> No extraordinary manifestation of the Spirit in tongues or similar gifts has come. Many of my friends have received such manifestations, but mine has still been a life of fellowship and service. At all times my spirit has been open to God for anything He might be pleased to reveal or bestow. But He has met me still with the old touch and spiritual sense, and in distinct and marked answers to believing prayer in my practical life.[23]

As recently as the preceding month (September 1912), Simpson had spent his ordination anniversary at Nyack "in a very solemn season of waiting" for God to bestow upon him Elisha's "double portion" of power.[24]

As evidence of Simpson's willingness to question further his earlier stance toward Pentecostalism, AG historian Carl Brumback cites a revealing conversation between Simpson and David McDowell (a one-time student at the Missionary Training Institute, later an AG executive, pastor, and evangelist), who returned to the Nyack campus in 1912. Presumably in the context of discussing Simpson's response to Pentecostalism, McDowell recollected him as having said: "David, I did what I thought was best, but I am afraid I missed it."[25] Were it not for the evidence of Simpson's diary, this anecdote preserved in the annals of Pentecostal history might readily be dismissed as obvious triumphalism. The diary's account of Simpson's unsuccessful pursuit of a Spirit baptism with tongues, however, apparently corroborates the revisionist comment attributed by McDowell to Simpson.

More insight into Simpson's attitude toward the Pentecostal experience of tongues, expressed as late as 1918 (the year before his death), can be gleaned from the writings of Carrie Judd Montgomery. A long-time intimate friend of the Simpsons, she stopped to visit them at Nyack on her tour through the eastern United States in 1918. In an atmosphere of what she described as "precious times of prayer and praise," Simpson reportedly reiterated his conviction that "the children of God in these solemn days should press on to receive all the fullness of

---

[23]Ibid., entry for October 6, 1912.
[24]Ibid.
[25]Brumback, *Sound*, 93–94.

the Spirit."[26] More significantly, he invited Montgomery, who had received a Spirit baptism with tongues in 1908 and by this time was an evangelist and missionary with the AG (since 1914), to speak at his traditional Friday afternoon meeting. In her words:

> I accepted Mr. Simpson's invitation to speak in one of his Friday afternoon meetings and was glad to tell them of the great things the Lord has done for me, not only in body, but also in mind and Spirit through the incoming, in all His fullness of the blessed Holy Ghost.[27]

Simpson's favorable disposition toward Montgomery's Pentecostal baptism is complemented by the final entry in his diary. It terminates in 1916 with an agonizing personal plea for the fullness of the Spirit to enable him to transcend besetting financial hardships, external opposition to the work of the Alliance, and new limitations imposed by the decline of his physical strength.[28] When Montgomery met with Simpson in 1918, he was recovering from a "nervous breakdown" that had lasted for nearly a year.[29] However, he still entertained the possibility of experiencing a greater baptism of the Spirit, even as his life was drawing to a close.

The image of Simpson as an obedient seeker of spiritual truth was a powerful inspiration to his followers. In an organization that more resembled a fraternity of otherworldly pilgrims pursuing a "higher" or "deeper" Christian life, the role of the leader as spiritual visionary was essential to its internal cohesion. For many persons, the experience of Spirit baptism with tongues was but another step in the journey that had first caused them to leave other religious bodies and join the Alliance. They did not, however, all agree as to whether this fourfold spiritual journey, now with an added fifth, "Pentecostal" stage, could best be continued inside or outside the organization.

Simpson's Followers—Those Who Left

The toleration in the Alliance for variant expressions of the Spirit-filled life, which Simpson both pleaded for and claimed

---

[26]Carrie Judd Montgomery: "An Eastern Trip in the Lord's Work," TF 39 (January 1919): 15; *Under His Wings* (Oakland: Stationers Corporation Printers, 1936), 231.

[27]Montgomery, *Under His Wings*, 231.

[28]See entry for October 14, 1916, in ND, 5.

[29]Montgomery, "Eastern Trip," 15.

existed, was insufficient for certain of his followers who looked for "new wineskins" to contain their "new Pentecostal wine." During the years 1907–15, the Alliance suffered the loss of numerous branch members, official workers, and missionaries to the Pentecostal movement.[30] Predictably the greatest number of departures occurred in the Ohio district and Indianapolis, Indiana, where the encounters between Pentecostals and other Alliance members were earliest and most intense.[31] Simpson keenly felt the resultant drain on human resources. He editorialized in 1913:

> We learn with deep sorrow that there is a quiet but continuous movement in a number of places, originating, we believe, in extreme leaders of what is known as the Pentecostal Movement, to turn away godly and useful members of the C&MA from their loyalty to the work and the faithful support of foreign mission workers for whom in many cases they have become responsible.[32]

Simpson's Episcopalian/Alliance associate, Kenneth Mackenzie, in a posthumous tribute, recalled poignantly the anguish of soul experienced by the Alliance leader as he witnessed the exodus of seasoned workers from his society:

> I cannot refrain from recording the agony through which he passed when so many of his most trusted and valued friends and workers withdrew from him because he did not go with them to the limit which was their ideal. He could not say of them, as did St. John, "They went out from us, but they were not of us," for they were. Their presence and prayers, their sympathy and service had been a bulwark to him in times of stress and strain.[33]

The normalization of tongues speaking in connection with Spirit baptism was the primary factor that brought about

---

[30]Alliance historian Robert B. Ekvall observed that the society's growth from 1897 to 1912 was "less rapid" due to the stress of the Pentecostal controversy and the demands of consolidation (*After Fifty Years*, 22).

[31]Alliance, Ohio, became the site of influential Pentecostal camp meetings in 1907 and 1908 in which Alliance persons of a Pentecostal persuasion participated. See Gary B. McGee's article, "Lupton, Levi Rakestraw (1860–1929)," DPCM, 561–62. William H. Piper states that twenty-five Alliance ministers withdrew from the Ohio district ("Notes," *Latter Rain Evangel* [July 1912]: 12).

[32]Simpson, "Editorial," AW 40 (September 6, 1913): 353.

[33]Kenneth Mackenzie as quoted in A. E. Thompson, *The Life of A. B. Simpson* (New York: Christian Alliance, 1920), 253.

schism in the ranks. While Simpson consistently defended on biblical grounds the legitimacy of the gift of tongues, both his experience of Spirit baptism and that of the Alliance collectively prior to 1907 had little direct exposure to charismatic manifestations immediately accompanying a "crisis experience" subsequent to conversion-regeneration. The sizeable number of Alliance persons who received a Spirit baptism with tongues during 1907 and 1908 posed a direct threat to the older, more quiescent experiential norm. The initial evidence doctrine was then later developed as the biblical rationalization for this nontraditional manner of receiving the Spirit. The lives of Daniel W. Kerr, David McDowell, William W. Simpson, Minnie T. Draper, George N. Eldridge, Claude A. McKinney, and Carrie Judd Montgomery illustrate well the process of Spirit baptism with tongues, separation, and doctrinal rationalization.

Daniel Kerr, a member of the famed Ohio Quartet, received his Spirit baptism with tongues in 1907 at the Beulah Park camp meeting near Cleveland, while pastoring the Alliance Tabernacle at Dayton. In 1911, he moved to pastor the Alliance church in Cleveland, which subsequently voted to become the Pentecostal Church of Cleveland, Ohio.[34] Much respected in the AG, Kerr distinguished himself as an ardent advocate of the initial evidence doctrine, which he saw as indispensable to the separate identity of the Pentecostal movement.[35] Since there was no controversy in the first century surrounding tongues speaking and its relationship to Spirit baptism, Kerr saw no need for the book of Acts to record uniformly the presence of tongues in every instance where believers were initially filled with the Spirit. The obvious did not require continuous repetition. He placed the burden of proof instead on those who questioned the normality of tongues speaking as the initial physical evidence of Spirit baptism.[36] In a

---

[34] For an account of Kerr's Pentecostal "baptism" and the subsequent course of his life, see Brumback, *Sound*, 76–78.

[35] Kerr, *Waters*, 39. In AG circles he was affectionately known as "Daddy Kerr." See Blumhofer, *The Assemblies of God: A Popular History*, 67.

[36] Kerr, *Waters*, 44–45; cf. Kerr's defense of the initial evidence doctrine in: "Do All Speak in Tongues?" CE (January 11, 1919): 7; "Paul's Interpretation of the Baptism in Holy Spirit," CE (August 24, 1918): 6; "The 'A' or 'An'—Which?" PE (January 21, 1922): 7; "Not Ashamed," PE (April 2, 1921): 5; "The Bible Evidence of the Baptism with the Holy Ghost," PE (August 11, 1923): 2–3. Others also regarded the initial evidence doctrine as crucial to Pentecostal identity. For example, see J. Roswell Flower's

stroke of historical irony, Kerr became embroiled in a controversy sparked by the AG healing evangelist Fred F. Bosworth, who contested the initial evidence doctrine and was in favor of allocating tongues to just one of the possible evidences of Spirit baptism. Bosworth subsequently resigned from the AG and affiliated with the Alliance, which Kerr had left.[37]

Similarly, David McDowell received his Spirit baptism with tongues in 1907 in an Alliance camp meeting at Rocky Springs Park, Lancaster, Pennsylvania.[38] As pastor of the Alliance mission in Waynesboro, Pennsylvania, he endeavored to propagate this experience among his flock through cottage prayer meetings.[39] His commitment to the experience of Spirit baptism with tongues, however, placed him on a journey of separation that eventually led into the AG, where he became a stalwart supporter of the initial evidence doctrine. For McDowell, the special privilege of the "last day of the outpouring of the Holy Spirit" was to be enabled to engage in "direct communication" with God in the "language of heaven."[40] He enthusiastically endorsed as "simply unanswerable" the arguments for tongues as the New Testament evidence of Spirit baptism articulated in Jonathan E. Perkins's book, *The Brooding Presence and Pentecost*.[41] Drawing from his own Alliance past, McDowell realized the camp meeting to be a highly effective vehicle for spiritual renewal, and thus helped reproduce the same type of setting for Pentecostals.[42]

---

comments to this effect in PE (April 17, 1920): 2. A lengthier discussion of Pentecostal conflict over the evidence doctrine appears in Anderson, *Vision*, 161–64.

[37]See R. M. Riss, "Bosworth, Fred F. (1877–1958)," DPCM, 94. For Bosworth's "Simpsonian" position on tongues, see Fred F. Bosworth, *Do All Speak with Tongues* (New York: Christian Alliance, n.d.); Eunice M. Perkins, *Joybringer Bosworth* (Dayton: John J. Scruby, 1921), 53–89.

[38] See the account of McDowell's Pentecostal "baptism" in Frodsham, *Signs*, 49–50; cf. the report of "many extra meetings" for inquiry and waiting on God in which several persons spoke in tongues at the Rocky Springs convention (CMAW 28 [September 7, 1907]: 116), and that the meetings were under "wise and cautious insight" (CMAW 28 [July 27, 1907]: 37).

[39]David H. McDowell, "Father and Son Healed Together," in *Touched by the Fire*, ed. Warner, 93.

[40]McDowell., "Communion with God," *Bridal Call* 3 (September 1919): 11.

[41]See McDowell's endorsement in Jonathan Elsworth Perkins, *The Brooding Presence and Pentecost*, 3d ed. (Springfield, Mo.: Gospel Publishing House, 1926), 8.

[42]*Bridal Call* 3 (September 1919): 20. McDowell arranged meetings

The case of William W. Simpson, though he was an over-seas missionary, was similar to that of Kerr and McDowell. Simpson (no relation to A. B. Simpson) had gone to southwest China as an Alliance missionary in 1892.[43] As a result of a revival accompanied by tongues that occurred among the Chinese and his missionary colleagues in early 1908, Simpson was persuaded of the need to be baptized in the Holy Spirit according to the pattern of Acts 2:4.[44] It was not until 1912, however, that he actually received his Spirit baptism with tongues, which was presaged in a "remarkable dream."[45] Simpson wrote of the resultant alienation and separation from other workers:

> Because we had all . . . received the Spirit and nearly 100 of the Chinese too received in the next year [1913], and all believed the teaching that the baptism in the Spirit is now just the same as at Pentecost, the other missionaries urged us to leave and we were finally forced to resign from the C&MA in Hankow, China, May 10, 1914.[46]

His path to separation was paved by a perception of A. B. Simpson and his co-workers on the field as being hostile to his new Pentecostal "baptism." In a strongly worded postseparation letter to A. B. Simpson dated October 17, 1916, W. W. Simpson challenged the Alliance founder and "many others in the Alliance" to stop

> fighting against God in turning down the teaching that the Lord baptized people in the Holy Spirit now just as He did on the

---

with Aimee Semple McPherson in July 1919, at the campgrounds near Scranton, Penn.

[43]See W. W. Simpson, "Holy Land," unpublished typed manuscript in the AG Collection, Myer Pearlman Memorial Library, Central Bible College, Springfield, Mo., July 30, 1953, 1; idem, "Adventures in Tibet," *The World Challenge* (September 1957): 6–7, 10.

[44]See W. W. Simpson's report of the revival in AR (1907–08): 127–28; idem, "This is That," PE (June 28, 1953): 5, 9, esp. 9. His account of the effect of the revival on him is in "A Martyred Missionary," unpublished typed manuscript in the AG Collection, Myer Pearlman Memorial Library, Central Bible College, Springfield, Mo., 2; cf. his "How the Holy Spirit Came to Northwest China," PE (December 31, 1950): 9.

[45]For an account of the dream, see W. W. Simpson, "Notes From Kansu," TF 33 (March 1913): 52–53. Other accounts by W. W. Simpson of his journey into Pentecostalism are reproduced in Edith L. Blumhofer, *Pentecost in My Soul* (Springfield, Mo.: Gospel Publishing House, 1989), 240–44.

[46]W. W. Simpson, "Martyred Missionary," 2; on the alleged opposition of the principal of the Alliance Bible School in China to tongues speaking, see idem, "Refuse Not Him That Speaketh," PE (November 17, 1945): 5.

day of Pentecost. . . . And if you will only humble yourself to seek the Lord for this mighty baptism, you'll get it and then you'll *know* what I am talking about.[47]

Almost twenty years after his "baptism," W. W. Simpson recalled the disinterest of his fellow Alliance missionaries in a Spirit baptism with tongues because of their teaching of what he termed an unscriptural "baptism of love."[48] The contemplative strain of A. B. Simpson's teaching that highlighted the importance of stillness in the Spirit-filled life also came under fire from W. W. Simpson. The ex-Alliance missionary chastised his former leader for the latter's overdependence on the "still small Voice," which he denounced as a regression to a "past dispensation."[49] An expectation of "the mighty sound of Pentecost," more in accord with the pattern of the book of Acts, "suited this age better."[50] After affiliating himself with the AG, W. W. Simpson, like Kerr and McDowell, became an outspoken apologist for the initial evidence doctrine.[51]

Minnie T. Draper, a long-time associate of Simpson best known for her healing ministry during Alliance conventions held at Rocky Springs, Pennsylvania, and Old Orchard, Maine, was another of those who eventually chose the path of separation. Originally a Presbyterian, she had deep spiritual roots in the Alliance. In Simpson's Gospel Tabernacle she had been both miraculously healed and "definitely sanctified."[52] Her views on divine healing closely resembled those of the Alliance founder.[53]

---

[47]W. W. Simpson to A. B. Simpson, May 12, 1914 (his emphasis). A copy of the letter is in the Canadian Bible College/Canadian Theological Seminary Archives in Regina, Saskatchewan. The original is attached to the executive committee minutes of the Alliance Board of Managers for June 13, 1914, 16.

[48]W. W. Simpson, "God's Purpose in This Generation," PE (June 27, 1931): 2.

[49]W. W. Simpson to A. B. Simpson, May 12, 1914.

[50]Ibid.

[51]See W. W. Simpson, "Why 'Tongues'?" PE (April 14, 1945): 3. On Simpson's controversial resignation from the Alliance over the extent to which Spirit baptism with tongues should be promoted and his later affiliation with the AG in 1918, see A. B. Simpson, "Editorial," AW 42 (May 30, 1914): 130; Robert H. Glover, "Conflicting Forces," AW 51 (October 5, 1918): 9; idem, "Good News from W. W. Simpson," CE (November 2, 1918): 11.

[52]Christian J. Lucas, "In Memoriam," *Full Gospel Missionary Herald Quarterly* 5 (April 1921): 3.

[53]See especially her views on the use of medicine: Minnie Draper,

As a zealous and highly effective ambassador of Simpson's Four-fold Gospel, Draper served for several years on the executive board of the Alliance until its reorganization in 1912.[54] For seven years after her Pentecostal baptism with tongues in 1906, she endeavored to retain her association with the Alliance while simultaneously identifying with the Pentecostal movement. Though still in the Alliance, she assisted in the establishment of Bethel Pentecostal Assembly in Newark, New Jersey (1907).[55]

Through her association with this influential indepen-dent Pentecostal congregation she left her stamp on early Pente-costal educational and missionary efforts.[56] A conflict of personal loyalties combined with the rising tide of anti-Pentecostal senti-ment in the Alliance ultimately led her to resign from the execu-tive board in 1912 and to sever completely her Alliance ties in 1913.[57] In the same year (1913) she was involved in the organi-zation of the Ossining Gospel Assembly, Ossining, New York. Ironically, apart from its propagation of the Pentecostal version of Spirit baptism according to Acts 2:4, the doctrine, structure, and ministry of this Pentecostal church were scarcely distinguish-able from that of an Alliance congregation.[58]

If Simpson was grieved by both the tension engendered in his society by Pentecostalism and the departure of veteran workers to join the new movement, those who left saw their

---

"A Threefold Prescription. James 4: 7, 8," TF 30 (January 1910): 15–16.

[54]See Gary B. McGee, "Draper, Minnie Tingley (1858–1921)," DPCM, 250.

[55]Lucas, "In Memoriam," 4.

[56]Draper's role as president of the "Bethel Board" in establishing the Pentecostal Mission in South and Central Africa (1910) and the Bethel Bible Training School (1916) is documented in Gary B. McGee, "Three Notable Women," AG *Heritage* 6 (Spring 1985–86): 4–5.

[57]See her letter of resignation to the secretary of the Christian and Missionary Alliance Board dated April 6, 1912, in her personal file in the A. B. Simpson Historical Library in Colorado Springs, Colo.; cf. McGee, "Draper," DPCM, 250.

[58]The stated objectives of the Ossining Gospel Assembly were "to provide for and conduct Divine worship and the moral improvement of mankind, religious, benevolent and missionary work in harmony with the following principles of the Christian religion: faith in Christ Jesus for the salvation of souls, sanctification of believers, Divine healing, Second Coming of Christ, and the Baptism of the Holy Spirit, according to the first and second chapter of the Book of Acts and as depicted in the second chapter of the Book of Joel." See "The Ossining Gospel Assembly," Ossin-ing, N.Y., 1974 (mimeographed), 3.

separation as the costly price of spiritual renewal. George N. Eldridge, who as a district superintendent had first opposed the seeking of Spirit baptism with tongues by members of his congregation in Indianapolis in 1907, was attracted to the Azusa Street meetings in 1910, after transferring to the Southern California District of the Alliance. Following his Spirit baptism with tongues and subsequent resignation from the organization in 1916, he founded and pastored Bethel Temple in Los Angeles.[59] Eldridge reflected on his transition to Pentecostalism in the light of his earlier entry into the Alliance through contact with Simpson, which had come after three years of Methodist ministry. In this first experience of separation, a veritable "Gethsemane in soul suffering," Eldridge recalled his dilemma as a choice "between obeying [his] beloved Church and obeying [his] Lord." He elected "to do the latter."[60] When his spiritual journey brought him to a second crossroads where he had to decide whether to remain with or leave the Alliance, similar feelings resurfaced: "We felt we must fully identify ourselves with the Pentecostal people, and again came a mighty struggle to sever our official relations with old friends."[61]

For Claude A. McKinney, a pastor and evangelist in Akron, Ohio, who received Spirit baptism with tongues in 1906 and withdrew from the Alliance in 1908, separation was embraced as a means to greater holiness. Though he did not regard leaving as an end in itself, McKinney saw departure as virtually unavoidable:

> When you step out for Pentecost you may lose some business, some friends and perhaps some standing in your church. But as you count the loss, God will take care of the credit side of your account up there.[62]

---

[59]See the notice of Eldridge's transfer to Southern California in "Editorial," CMAW 27 (June 29, 1907): 301. Regarding his continued Alliance loyalty at that time, see his report "South Pacific District," in AR (1907–08): 76–77. For other biographical facts, see George N. Eldridge, *Personal Reminiscences* (Los Angeles: West Coast Publishing Co., n.d.), 40–41; Stanley H. Frodsham, "Dr. G. N. Eldridge with the Lord," PE (February 22, 1930): 12; L. F. Wilson, "Eldridge, George N. (1847–1930)," DPCM, 259; Carrie Judd Montgomery, "Our Visit in Los Angeles," TF 36 (April 1916): 86.

[60]Eldridge, *Reminiscences*, 38–40; cf. 41 for his account of receiving Spirit baptism with tongues "during the night watches."

[61]Ibid., 42. In 1919, Eldridge invited Aimee Semple McPherson to conduct meetings in his church. See McPherson's mention of the invitation in *Bridal Call* 2 (February 1919): 15–16, followed by a report of the success of the meetings.

[62]Claude A. McKinney, "Our Righteousness in Him," *Bridal Call* 3

In his estimation, much of the "separating" came over public tongues speaking.[63] What was lamented by Simpson as needless schism, arising out of biblically unsound doctrine, to McKinney was God "calling a people through His Spirit and making a selection from a selection."[64]

The restorationism preached by Simpson as the historical legitimization for his Fourfold Gospel was simply accepted and adapted by those who left to suit their new Pentecostal agenda. Like their former leaders, they articulated the thesis that lost apostolic truth was recovered from the sixteenth to the nineteenth centuries. Unlike the Alliance, however, which built largely on already recovered truth, they saw Pentecostalism as advancing significantly the restoration process; hence the need for Pentecostals to separate from other religious bodies. After crediting Luther and Wesley with restoring justification by faith and holiness to the church, and Blumhardt and Trüdel with the revival of divine healing and premillennialism, Daniel Kerr concluded:

> In latter years there have been other spiritual movements but with no essentially new doctrines. Dr. A. B. Simpson brought forward the truth that the Lord Jesus was not only our Physician, but our life. His testimony was summed up in that beautiful hymn: "Once it was the blessing, now it is the Lord."
>
> During the past few years God has enabled us to discover and recover this wonderful truth concerning the Baptism in the Spirit as it was given at the beginning. Thus we have all that the others got, and we have got this too. We see all they see, but they don't see what we see.
>
> That is why we can't work together with those who oppose or reject this Pentecostal truth. . . . Some have tried and failed.[65]

The willingness to transfer one's religious loyalties was, for Kerr, the proof of one's preparedness to follow God and be part of God's pilgrim people. He continued:

(October 1919): 16–17. On his early withdrawal from the Alliance and later affiliation with the AG, see G. W. Gohr, "McKinney, Claude Adams (1873–1940)," DPCM, 567.

[63]McKinney, "Our Righteousness in Him," 17.

[64]Ibid.; cf. his article, "Adam Where Art Thou," *Bridal Call* 3 (April 1920): 10–11, in which McKinney explains salvation as a calling from religious formalism to a life of intimate communion with God, which he found in Pentecostalism.

[65]Daniel W. Kerr, "The Basis for Our Distinctive Testimony," PE (September 2, 1922): 4.

> We want to be ready, like the children of Israel, so that just as soon as the cloud lifts and begins to move we will pull up our little tents of experience. . . . And if His people want His presence they must be on the move.

> We call this the Pentecostal "m-o-v-e-m-e-n-t." Years ago there was the Alliance "movement" and before that there was the holiness "movement." Why "movement?" Because God is on the *move*. Beloved we are a *moving* people.[66]

Further justifying his separation from the Alliance, Kerr redirected the familiar Simpson cliché, "Once it was the blessing, now it is the Lord," against his former organization. The Alliance was now the people of the "blessing" and Pentecostals, the people of "the Lord, the Blesser."[67]

Even though the end result of their "Pentecostalized" spiritual journey was one of eventual separation, there were those who endeavored to maintain amicable relations with their former colleagues. Carrie Judd Montgomery, a minister-teacher, author, editor, director of faith homes, and social worker, was one such person.[68] Few had been closer to Simpson. She was connected with his inner circle from the beginning in 1887, and organized an Oakland branch in 1891.[69] At her marriage ceremony in 1890, Simpson read two bridal poems in her honor, one of which he composed specially for the occasion.[70] He later dedi-

---

[66]Kerr, "The Practice of the Presence of God," PE (February 14, 1925): 3 (his emphasis). The same restorationist motif is enunciated by others of Kerr's former "Alliance" colleagues in the AG. See W. I. Evans, "This River Must Flow," PE (August 3, 1946): 2; J. Roswell Flower, "The Present Position of Pentecost," PE (June 13, 1925): 7. There are hints of it in J. W. Welch's testimony, "The Power of Apostolic Days for You in the Twentieth Century," PE (November 1, 1919): 2–3.

[67]Kerr, "Practice," 2.

[68]For an insightful overview of the faith healing/Alliance/Pentecostal phases of her life, see Daniel E. Albrecht, "Carrie Judd Montgomery: Pioneering Contributor to Three Religious Movements," Pneuma 8 (Fall 1986): 101–19; cf. W. E. Warner, "Montgomery, Carrie Judd (1858–1946)," DPCM, 626–28.

[69]See Carrie Judd Montgomery: Under His Wings, 143; "Old Orchard Convention," TF 7 (September 1887): 203–4; "All the Way," TF 42 (February 1922): 36–37; and her annual reports as recording secretary of the Christian Alliance in TF 8 (November 1888): 241–44; TF 10 (April 1890): 82–84. Regarding her founding of the Oakland Alliance Branch, see Under His Wings, 143; "The Work and the Workers," TF 11 (December 1891): 274–75.

[70]Montgomery, Under His Wings, 132–34, esp. 133–34.

cated Montgomery's child at the New York Gospel Tabernacle in 1892.[71] In view of her own similar experience of divine healing, he gave her considerable public exposure in his conventions.[72] In Montgomery's eulogy of Simpson, she spoke of her thirty-eight-year relationship with him and of the

> many tender memories that came thronging to our mind as we [she and her husband] review his life, and work, and what his life and influence have meant to us personally.[73]

A few years later she expressed her indebtedness more specifically to the Alliance founder:

> I can never express my gratitude to God for Mr. Simpson's fatherly kindness to me and the wise way in which he was used of God to lead me out in more prominent platform work than I had before attempted.[74]

Montgomery treasured the Christian Alliance as a source of "blessed fellowship" for those "pioneers" (like Simpson and herself) in the holiness and healing movements who had "met much rebuff along the lines of the deeper truths."[75]

After her Spirit baptism with tongues in 1908, she promoted Pentecostal themes in the *Triumphs of Faith*, which she edited, but not at the expense of either her Fourfold Gospel consciousness or her Alliance relationships.[76] Testimonies of her Pentecostal "baptism" were synthesized with the Alliance emphasis on holy stillness, divine healing, growth in sanctification, and discernment.[77] Her criticisms of an exaggerated accentuation of tongues strikingly resembled Simpson's own cautions.[78]

---

[71]Ibid., 146.

[72]Montgomery, "All the Way," 36–37.

[73]Montgomery, "The Passing of a Great and Good Man," TF 39 (November 1919): 253.

[74]Montgomery, "All the Way," 36–37.

[75]Ibid., 37.

[76]For her promotion of the experience of Spirit baptism with tongues, see Carrie Judd Montgomery: "The Promise of the Father," TF 28 (July 1908): 145–49; "Speaking in Tongues," TF 30 (November 1910): 253–55; *Secrets of Victory* (Oakland: Office of Triumphs of Faith, 1921), 136–43; *Under His Wings*, 164–70.

[77]For examples of a marriage of Pentecostal and Alliance themes in her writing, see Montgomery: "A Year with the Comforter," TF 29 (July 1909): 145–49; "Who Redeemeth Thy Life from Destruction," TF 40 (March 1920): 48–52; "Forty-five Years of Blessing and Service," TF 44 (January 1924): 35.

[78]See Montgomery, "A Year With the Comforter," 147; cf. her

Montgomery's missionary itinerary around the world in 1909 wove in and out of Alliance and Pentecostal contexts. It was indicative of her desire to cultivate a peaceful coexistence between these phases of her life.[79] Her post-1908 Pentecostal affinities did not preclude a continuation of her platform presence in the Alliance.

Upon returning to the United States, she first stayed at the Alliance guest house in New York and subsequently engaged in public ministry in two of Simpson's services and four conventions. At Old Orchard, Simpson even adjusted the daily schedule to make room for her participation.[80] She utilized all of these opportunities to share her Pentecostal experience.[81] In the course of her travels, she visited both Alliance and Pentecostal friends. Again, during a 1918 trip to the eastern United States, a decade after her Pentecostal "baptism," Montgomery (as mentioned earlier) visited with the Simpsons and spoke in his Friday afternoon meeting.[82] Her advocacy of the Pentecostal message and affiliation with the AG had evidently not diminished the Alliance founder's respect and affection for her.[83]

---

initial reservations toward Pentecostalism because of extremist elements (which paralleled Simpson's criticisms) in "The Promise of the Father," 145–46. On the need for order and decorum in public worship services, see Montgomery, "Pentecostal Conference," TF 39 (July 1909): 152.

[79]For a description of her Alliance and Pentecostal itinerary, see *Under His Wings*, 171–85.

[80]Ibid., 186–87. Montgomery indicates she spoke on "the Holy Spirit's fullness, divine healing and kindred subjects." For her attendance at and involvement in other Alliance services, conventions, and Simpson's services, see the entries for July 3, 4, 5, 25, 26, 30, 31; August 1, 2, 3, 4, 6, 7, 8, 14, 15, 16, 17, 29; September 5, 1909, in her personal diary. A copy of the diary is in the AG Archives in Springfield, Mo. Cf. Montgomery's articles: "Here and There," TF 30 (July 1910): 145–47; "Days of Service and Blessing," TF 30 (September 1910): 193–96; "Service for the King," TF 30 (October 10, 1910): 217–20.

[81]See her "Letters from Mrs. Montgomery," TF 29 (August 1909): 175–78; "Old Orchard Convention," TF 29 (August 1909): 178; "Letters from Mrs. Montgomery," TF 29 (September 1909): 207.

[82]On this trip Montgomery met some of her former Alliance friends, besides the Simpsons, but for the most part she followed a "Pentecostal" itinerary. See her "Eastern Trip," 12–17, esp. 15; idem, *Under His Wings*, 230–32, esp. 231.

[83]Montgomery first acquired credentials from the AG in 1917, though she did hold a certificate of ordination with the Churches of God in Christ (dated January 11, 1914) prior to the birth of the AG. See her personal file in the AG Archives, Springfield, Mo.

Carrie Judd Montgomery's posture toward the Alliance after receiving her Spirit baptism with tongues at fifty years of age was determined more by the natural flow of events and the gradual evolution of her entrepreneurial life than by a deliberate separatist strategy on her part. For ten years after her Pentecostal "baptism," she continued to exercise an informal leadership role in the Alliance. Her personal ties to Simpson were deep. Moreover, her appreciation for the Fourfold Gospel was enriched, not reduced, by the experience of Spirit baptism with tongues. Furthermore, the interdenominational, missionary character of the Alliance made it possible for her to remain active in it while at the same time serving as an ordained minister of the AG—a rarity, given the growing polarization of the two movements.

Montgomery never became a doctrinaire separatist, as did Daniel Kerr and others. Daniel Albrecht has aptly described her as a "bridge-builder" between Pentecostals and non-Pentecostals.[84] Though she subscribed to the initial evidence doctrine, the separatist overtones of this distinctive were tempered by the larger, overarching themes of love and Christian unity that defined her life and ministry.[85] The winsome, nonsectarian manner in which she disseminated her unique blend of Alliance and Pentecostal teaching gave her credibility in both camps. Montgomery embodied Simpson's spirit of evangelical ecumenism, a feature of her life that endeared her to both constituencies. From 1908 to 1918, when the Alliance recoiled from Pentecostal fanaticism, and Pentecostals, strengthened by Alliance additions, began to develop separate denominational identities, Montgomery tried to integrate what she perceived to be the best of both movements. Her writings were remarkably free of unwholesome polemic in either direction, and her consistently charitable dis-

---

[84]See Albrecht's brief but interesting discussion of Montgomery's efforts to bring holiness and Pentecostal people together in mutual understanding at a time when a deep rift was developing between the movements ("Carrie Judd Montgomery," 111–12).

[85]On the priority of love in Montgomery's spirituality, see her articles: "Knit Together in Love," TF 28 (September 1908): 193–95; "By This Shall All Men Know," TF 28 (November 1908): 241; "A Year with the Comforter," TF 29 (July 1909): 148; "Service for the King," TF 30 (October 1910): 220. Montgomery's commitment to Christian unity is reflected in her article "Edifying the Body of Christ" (TF 32 [June 1902]: 121–22), and in her holding of ecumenical "Monday meetings" in Oakland in 1911 (see Under His Wings, 196–97).

position overrode any separatist impulse that might have been generated by her association with the Pentecostal movement. At her funeral service conducted at the Alliance Tabernacle in Oakland in 1946, the Pentecostal eulogist commenced by paying tribute to Montgomery's ecumenical life, which transcended "any particular section of the world or . . . any particular denomination." He then proceeded to claim her for his own movement as a "firm believer" in the "initial evidence" doctrine who "did not regard it as a tenet to be carnally contended for, or . . . carnally rejected or set aside."[86]

Finally, the manner in which those who left responded to the public denunciations of the dubious personalities and spurious elements within the Pentecostal movement merits consideration. They were not oblivious to the dangers of extremism. In this sense they concurred with Alliance concerns expressed most frequently during a period from 1907 to 1909. However, what for Alliance critics constituted errors serious enough to distance them from Pentecostalism were for these former associates of Simpson matters deserving of pastoral correction that neither discredited the movement nor undermined their decision to identify with it. Daniel Kerr countered the preoccupation of evangelical opponents with the radical fringes by observing that

> there has never been a real spiritual movement in which there could not be found objectionable conditions and practices; people of extreme and fanatical tendencies; strange and weird manifestations; and insubordinate and lawless persons who disregarded all laws of Christian courtesy and decency.[87]

Caricaturing Pentecostalism according to its most undesirable elements, to Kerr, amounted to an excuse fabricated by those on the "outside" who were unwilling to go beyond "the surface of the Scripture into the deeper strata of revelation touching the real crux of the movement."[88] Their distorted perspectives were in reality "reproaches of the cross" to be endured by Pentecostals, whom he exhorted to hold unwaveringly to their distinctive testimony of Spirit baptism with tongues. Aligning oneself with "any spiritual movement," for Kerr, invariably meant being exposed to

---

[86]See the copy of the address by J. Narver Gortner, "Carrie Judd Montgomery—A Tribute," which is in the AG Archives, Springfield, Mo.

[87]See Kerr, *Waters*, 37.

[88]Ibid.

"pressures from without and from within."[89] The "rule" of past spiritual movements amply bore out his claim. If Pentecostals succumbed to what he dubbed a "propaganda of intrigue," spread by "old and well-established religious organizations," then Pentecostalism as a renewing force within the church would decline and eventually die.[90]

While Kerr primarily redressed the external critics of Pentecostalism, David W. Myland, who had previously been the Alliance superintendent for the Ohio district from 1898 to 1904, pastored the congregation in Columbus, Ohio, and sung in the Ohio Quartet, labored to curb Pentecostal excesses from within.[91] After receiving a Spirit baptism with tongues in 1906, Myland continued to preach the Pentecostal message within the Alliance until sometime in 1911 or 1912, when he left to join the new movement.[92] Though he never formally affiliated with the AG, his more than twenty years of Alliance leadership experience proved a stabilizing influence among early Pentecostals.[93]

While Myland's positive stance on the initial evidence doctrine was uncompromising, he nevertheless objected strenuously to any overemphasis on tongues speaking. In an article entitled "The Fulness and Effects of Pentecost," published in 1909, Myland, with Pentecostal extremists in mind, wrote:

> Now I am no modifier of tongues, please remember that, nor am I a stickler about tongues; you never had any too much tongues for me, but I will not, I cannot, and I shall not magnify tongues out of its legitimate, its scriptural setting and its value compared with other gifts of the Spirit. Tongues is the least of

[89]Ibid., 37–38.

[90]Ibid., 36.

[91]Myland's life has been rescued from the obscurity imposed upon him by early Alliance historians in J. Kevin Butcher's study, "The Holiness and Pentecostal Labors of David Wesley Myland 1890–1918" (M.Th. thesis, Dallas Theological Seminary, 1983); cf. E. B. Robinson's article, "Myland, David Wesley (1858–1943)," DPCM, 632–33.

[92]During an Alliance convention in Columbus, Myland experienced his Spirit baptism with tongues as well as a healing from acute burns and blood poisoning; see his account in D. Wesley Myland, *The Latter Rain Covenant and Pentecostal Power with Testimony of Healings and Baptism*, 2d ed. (1910; reprint, Chicago: Evangel Publishing House, 1911), 153f., esp. 160. On the problematic date of Myland's departure from the Alliance see Butcher, "Myland," 125 n. 65.

[93]See Butcher's conclusion regarding many of Myland's unsung contributions in "Myland," 130–37.

all the gifts and subordinate to other gifts, and when it is not kept so, there is some trouble.[94]

Myland echoed Simpson in both his insistence on an orderly use of the gift in public worship and his linking of Spirit baptism to an ongoing experience of inner peacefulness.[95] In what is the only scholarly study to date of Myland's contributions to the holiness and Pentecostal movements, J. Kevin Butcher has convincingly shown Myland to have been one of those individuals who epitomized the best of spiritual integrity and scholarship in early Pentecostalism, in contradistinction to some of the "charlatanry, phony-emotionalism, and shoddy, uneducated, biblical interpretation" that dogged the movement.[96]

Simpson's Followers—Those Who Stayed

Though many of those persons in the Alliance who experienced a Spirit baptism with tongues chose to identify themselves with the new Pentecostal movement, some notable followers of Simpson opted for continuing their spiritual journeys within the tradition of the Fourfold Gospel. For various reasons, their "baptism" did not create an impetus to separate.

The case of Simpson's Canadian associate, John Salmon (1831–1918), deserves consideration in this respect. Somewhat analogous to Simpson's, Salmon's theological and spiritual development was eclectic. Prior to his initial contact with Simpson in 1885, Salmon's ecclesiastical life had gone through Presbyterian, Methodist, Adventist, Congregational, and Baptist phases.[97] His personal relationship with Simpson, which lasted over thirty-two years, was first cemented through a healing that he received in 1885 from a terminal kidney disease, during a divine healing convention Simpson conducted at Buffalo.[98]

---

[94]David W. Myland, "The Fulness and Effects of Pentecost," *Latter Rain Evangel* (September 1909): 16.

[95]Ibid., 17.

[96]Butcher, "Myland," 6.

[97]See Lindsay Reynolds, *Footprints. The Beginnings of the Christian and Missionary Alliance in Canada* (Beaverlodge, Alberta: Buena Books, 1981), 1–60, for Salmon's pre-Alliance ecclesiastical experiences.

[98]See Salmon's description of his healing and Simpson's methodology in "Testimony," CMAW 24 (March 24, 1900): 185; and "God's Goodness to Me," AW 49 (December 29, 1917): 198–99.

Through the vicissitudes of his pre-Alliance journey, Salmon came independently to affirm the themes of the Fourfold Gospel. He was also attracted to the interdenominational, congregationally oriented polity later reflected in the organizational framework of the Alliance. His experience of divine healing at the Buffalo convention was the last step in a pilgrimage that brought him to identify with Simpson's vision. Given the direction that his own spiritual quest had taken him and his dedication to evangelizing unchurched, neglected masses, Salmon was a providentially prepared soulmate for Simpson. In 1887, the relationship was formalized when he was appointed one of the founding vice-presidents of the Christian Alliance, a position he held for a record twenty-five consecutive years.[99] Two years later, Salmon assumed the influential position of vice-president of the Dominion Auxiliary Branch of the Christian Alliance in Canada.[100]

Salmon received his Pentecostal "enduement" with tongues at the Beulah Park, Ohio, convention in August 1907, when he was seventy-five years of age. Shortly after, he retold the event in Simpson's magazine:

> There at an all-night of prayer I received another gracious visitation of the wonderful power of the Holy Spirit. About three o'clock in the morning one said to me that we had better retire to rest. I replied to the effect that I would remain till four o'clock. Shortly after that a power came upon me as I was bended lowly in prayer and praise . . . I continued for a length of time repeating over and over again: "Glory to Jesus, Glory to Jesus," till by and by I got down on the straw covering the ground of the Tabernacle. There I remained conscious all the time, but shaking a good deal and uttering a few words in a tongue to me unknown.[101]

Salmon interpreted this occurrence as the authentication of a baptism of the Holy Spirit that he had received almost two years earlier in Toronto after attending a deeper life convention at Simpson's Tabernacle in New York City. Far from allowing tongues speaking to invalidate all preceding spiritual crises in his life, Salmon theologized this experience simply as "another step fur-

---

[99]Reynolds, *Footprints*, 96.

[100] Ibid., 111–12.

[101] John Salmon, "My Enduement," CMAW 29 (October 26, 1907): 55.

ther" in a journey that promised more to come.[102] While there is no indication that Salmon ever subscribed to the initial evidence doctrine, he did actively propagate the Pentecostal baptism in Alliance circles.[103] The constitution of Bethany Chapel, which he founded in 1891 in Toronto, contained restorationist nuances that tied the historical loss and recovery of spiritual gifts to the spiritual condition of the church.[104] No doubt Salmon's episode of tongues speaking at Beulah Park, Ohio, further convinced him of the rightness of his church's constitution composed fifteen years previously.

Though Salmon was a staunch devotee of the Fourfold Gospel, there is some evidence that his Alliance loyalties wavered for a period of time as he was drawn to Pentecostalism.[105] In 1908 he was present at the first Pentecostal convention, which convened in Toronto.[106] After retiring from active involvement in the Canadian Alliance in 1911, Salmon relocated to Los Angeles. Freed from the demands of his previous office, he became again a free-spirited spiritual seeker and built closer ties with Pentecostals, only to become disenchanted with their excesses. Thus he returned wholeheartedly to the Alliance fold, much to the relief of his friends.[107] The ultimate fate of Bethany Chapel bore witness to its founder's mixed Alliance and Pentecostal sympathies. After the church was finally closed in 1929, the proceeds from the eventual sale of its property were divided between the

---

[102] Ibid., 54; "Baptized with the Holy Ghost," TF 28 (November 1908): 260.

[103] In her "Letter From Mrs. Montgomery," TF 29 (September 1909): 207, Carrie Judd Montgomery mentioned that Salmon and Mr. and Mrs. Daniel Kerr assisted her in praying for "hungry" persons to receive the Pentecostal baptism at the Beulah Park, Ohio, convention in 1909. Cf. Montgomery, Under His Wings, 187. Reynolds, Footprints, 289–90, maintains that Salmon never "preached 'tongues' from the pulpit of Bethany Chapel."

[104] The full text of the constitution is given in Reynolds, Footprints, 518–27; cf. 520.

[105] Membership in Salmon's Bethany Chapel required a more clear-cut commitment to the Fourfold Gospel than in Simpson's Gospel Tabernacle. See the Gospel Tabernacle's constitution and bylaws, which are silent on adherence to the Fourfold Gospel as a prerequisite for membership, in Year Book of the Christian Alliance and the International Missionary Alliance (1893) (New York: Christian Alliance, 1893), 41–43.

[106] Kulbeck, What God, 109.

[107] Eldridge, Reminiscences, 41.

Alliance and the Pentecostal Assemblies of Canada.[108] As John Salmon had lived, so Bethany Chapel died.

Robert Jaffray (1873–1945), the Canadian Alliance's premier missionary statesman in the twentieth century, emerges as the most illustrious example of those who saw no need to terminate service because of their experience of Spirit baptism with tongues. In the annals of Alliance history, there are few, if any, who more completely embodied in their life and ministry the tenets of the Fourfold Gospel. He was perhaps Simpson's most impressive disciple. Having first consecrated himself to Christian service under the influence of Simpson's preaching, Jaffray studied at the Missionary Training Institute, was ordained in Salmon's Bethany Chapel with Simpson present, served repeatedly as field chairman in South China, and spearheaded missions into Indochina and the Dutch East Indies.[109]

In October 1907, Jaffray, along with the other missionaries in Wuchow, South China, received a baptism of the Holy Spirit that for some of them (including Jaffray) involved speaking in tongues.[110] For him, his experience was perfectly compatible with the restorationist expectations instilled in him by his mentors. In his report of 1908 (for 1907), he surmised that the "great Spiritual revival" needed to effect an awakening in China could not happen unless the church was first bestowed with the "old Pentecostal power and gifts promised so long ago, but lost for [many] centuries."[111] The Pentecostal visitation of 1907 in South China, with its accompanying manifestations of tongues and healings, was recommended by Jaffray to the North American Alliance constituency as the fulfillment of the Old Testament "latter rain" prophecy in Zechariah 10:1.[112]

---

[108] Reynolds, *Footprints*, 301–2.

[109] The only biography of Jaffray is A. W. Tozer's seriously inadequate *Let My People Go* (Camp Hill: Christian Publications, 1948).

[110] See Jaffray's report in "South China," AR (1907–08): 143, and his article, "Speaking in 'Tongues'—Some Words of Kindly Counsel," CMAW 31 (March 13, 1909): 395. See Philip Hinkey, "Spiritual Awakening in South China," CMAW 28 (July 6, 1907): 318, for the expectation that a Pentecostal revival similar to that in India (1906) would also occur in South China. A report also appeared in the Pentecostal publication, *Apostolic Faith* 2 (May 1908): 4.

[111] Jaffray, "South China," 142; cf. Jaffray, "Tongues," 395.

[112] Jaffray, "South China," 142.

Jaffray openly rejoiced in the "anointing" with tongues that he and others had received in Wuchow. In an article entitled " 'Speaking in Tongues'—Some Words of Kindly Counsel," published in 1909, he enumerated the personal benefits derived from this experience: (1) a deeper love for and comprehension of the Scriptures; (2) an unconditional acknowledgment of personal weakness and the compensating power of the name and blood of Christ in prayer; (3) an increase in evangelistic unction; (4) sanctification in speech; and (5) a more mature discernment of the end-time activities of the Holy Spirit and evil spirits.[113] His assessment of Pentecostalism as a movement, however, resonated with Simpson's already voiced criticisms. Jaffray warned against the "extravagances and fanaticism" and counterfeit tongues that could issue from Pentecostals' fixation with the supernatural.[114] Further, he frowned upon "prolonged, special, waiting meetings" because of their potential for behavioral excesses where prudent leadership was lacking.[115]

In his elaboration on Pentecostal liabilities, he listed as "danger lines" of the movement: a spiritual elitism that resulted in sectarian tendencies, the undue elevation of spiritual gifts at the expense of biblical authority, the loss of evangelistic concern for the heathen because of an overindulgence in personal blessing, and the naive assumption of some missionaries that the gift of tongues would substitute for foreign language study.[116] His foremost objection to the Pentecostal movement (like Simpson's) pertained to the initial evidence doctrine, which had done incalculable injury to the church. Stating his disapproval of this teaching, Jaffray underscored that some of his fellow Alliance missionaries who were "most wonderfully baptized" and "most profoundly blessed" in Wuchow never spoke in tongues.[117]

Writing from the relative security of his overseas posting, Jaffray publicly moved further in a Pentecostal direction than did Simpson. Though opposed to the doctrine of tongues as the sole initial sign of Spirit baptism, he did concede that the thrust of the book of Acts pointed to tongues as a normative accompaniment

---

[113] Jaffray, "Tongues," 395.
[114] Ibid.
[115] Ibid., 396.
[116] Ibid., 395–96, 406.
[117] Ibid., 396.

of Spirit baptism. In a surprising departure from Simpson (who never spoke in tongues) Jaffray wrote:

> it should never be forgotten that while last in the Epistle it [tongues] is the first in order of experience in the Acts. May it not be that the Spirit usually gives the "tongues" first to test us and see whether or not we may be trusted with greater gifts of the Spirit which may be indeed of more value in the Christian ministry.[118]

He also aimed pointed words at ultraconservative voices in the Alliance who discounted any validity in the Pentecostal experience because of abuses present in the movement:

> There is a great danger, too of fearing the works of the devil to such an extent that we shall loose [sic] all courage to seek earnestly for the true and full endowment of the Spirit for which our souls hunger. I have met some who are so prejudiced on account of what they have seen that they say they have no desire to ever speak in tongues, forgetting that "tongues" is one of the "gifts of the Spirit." Let us not allow the enemy so to drive us away from, and cheat us out of the real blessings of the Spirit because he has counterfeited in some cases "the gift of tongues." We have no business to be afraid of evil spirits, for He has given us "power over all power of the enemy," and He can give supernatural discernment of spirits.[119]

Moreover, in Jaffray's opinion, "crudities and unusual manifestations" could "hardly be avoided" in times of spiritual visitation.[120] Those who had never been present in an atmosphere pregnant with the sense of the immediacy of the supernatural realm could never know the increased personal vulnerability of the moment. He harked back to his own situation:

> Some of us who were glad indeed when the wind blew, were glad also when the lull came, so that we could . . . get our bearings again. It is very easy for one who has had no such experience to coldly criticize one's actions who is under the power, but he knows nothing of what it means till he has himself realized the power of God.[121]

---

[118] Ibid., 395. Pentecostal historian Edith L. Blumhofer appears to miss this nuance in her discussion of Jaffray's article (*Assemblies*, 1:186–87).

[119] Jaffray, "Tongues," 395.

[120] Ibid., 396.

[121] Ibid., 406.

Though a year and a half had passed since his Pentecostal experience, Jaffray was still positively disposed to the private and public practice of tongues. His personal anointing continued unabated, and he supported the use of tongues in public meetings in accordance with 1 Corinthians 12 and 14.[122] If fully known, Jaffray's missionary career might well have been the envy of Pentecostals. A perusal of both his general correspondence and his overseas publications *The South China Alliance Tidings* and *The Pioneer* reveals that though he never left the Alliance, his life contained all the supernatural dimensions held dear by Pentecostals— tongues speaking, healings, signs and wonders, dreams and visions, numerous instances of direct divine guidance, and a commitment to training Spirit-baptized church leaders.[123] Jaffray's grafting of his Pentecostal "baptism" onto his Alliance heritage produced a spiritual profile with a rhythmic blend of evangelical, charismatic, and contemplative motifs.

Unlike Jaffray, who apparently never wavered from his Alliance commitments while absorbing what he deemed the best of Pentecostal spirituality, other missionaries showed considerably more vacillation. Harry L. Turner, a former Nyack student and Alliance missionary to Argentina, received the Pentecostal baptism with tongues and resigned from the Alliance in 1918.[124] During the "gap" in his record of Alliance service, he labored as both a Pentecostal missionary to Argentina and as pastor of Wesley Pentecostal Church in Winnipeg, Manitoba. Turner, however, later resurfaced in Alliance circles. Regaining his Alliance credibility through a succession of influential appointments, he emerged as the fifth president of the Alliance in 1954, a position he occupied until 1960.[125]

---

[122] Ibid., 395.

[123] For an excellent original survey of the charismatic dimensions of Jaffray's life, see Louise Green, "Robert Jaffray: Man of Spirit, Man of Power," *His Dominion* 16 (March 1990): 2–14.

[124] See McGee, *This Gospel*, 1:130–31.

[125] On Turner's Pentecostal activities see Kulbeck, *What God*, 144, 222. For his Alliance career, see Robert Niklaus et al., *All for Jesus*, 211–12, esp. 212, which describes Turner's Pentecostal sojourn as "a gap." Turner's pneumatological views are set forth in *The Voice of the Spirit* (Harrisburg: Christian Publications, 1951). See esp. 59–67, 119–25, 126–30, 131–39, 140–45, 146–48 for indications of his movement away from Pentecostalism back to Alliance "orthodoxy."

In summary, Simpson's example of being a diligent seeker of spiritual truth left an indelible impression on many of his followers, some of whom were prepared to continue their journey under a Pentecostal rather than an Alliance banner. The manner of relating the experience of Spirit baptism with tongues to the tradition of the Fourfold Gospel was expressed in a variety of personal scenarios. For the most part, the decision to remain within or to depart hinged on the relative strength of an individual's adherence to the initial evidence doctrine. Other factors also contributed significantly to the choices people made. If Pentecostalism, in its essence, were perceived as an aberration of those "restored" truths inherent to the Alliance, then a stereotype of Pentecostalism as more bane than boon to the church prevailed. The wariness induced by this cautious, critical mind-set defused any desire to join the new movement. If, however, the Pentecostal movement as a whole, despite its excesses, were viewed as a further stage in the divinely orchestrated process of restoring lost apostolic truth to the church, then separation was more likely. Such conduct, grievous as it was to Simpson, was consistent with his restorationist "spirit," if not his doctrinal "letter."

It cannot be said on the basis of the available evidence that Alliance workers of Pentecostal persuasion were officially forced out of the society. By 1914, however, the doctrinal and experiential boundaries within the organization were clearly demarcated. In February 1914, Simpson editorialized that Spirit baptism was to be intentionally differentiated from spiritual gifts. Though the Alliance had gone through a turbulent period as a result of its encounter with Pentecostalism, the spiritual gifts were still "fully recognized" and welcome in Alliance assemblies, provided they were exercised with humility, a sense of order and propriety, and a demonstrable regard for corporate edification.[126] A few months later, the Alliance enunciated its official position, which concurred with Simpson's previously held position on Spirit baptism, spiritual gifts, and the initial evidence doctrine. In accord with the apostolic precedent, the Board of Managers accepted that tongues speaking and other miraculous phenomena could "accompany or follow" the baptism of the Holy Spirit, but

---

[126]Simpson, "Editorial," AW 41 (February 14, 1914): 305. The issue also contained an article by Simpson, "The Overshadowing of the Holy Spirit," which dealt with the full-orbed ministry of the Holy Spirit (ibid., 306–8, 311).

they were not endemic to it. Other ways of receiving the fullness of the Holy Spirit were deemed equally legitimate. Any attempt to promulgate tongues as the exclusive initial confirmation of Spirit baptism was in violation of the "exceedingly plain" teaching of 1 Corinthians 12–14.[127]

Still pained by the division that Pentecostalism fomented among Alliance workers, Simpson continued to insist that the "fullest liberty" was extended to Pentecostals in the Alliance to "receive and exercise all the gifts of the Spirit." In return, he asked for a similarly accommodating spirit to be exhibited toward those who knew certainly the Spirit's fullness, but could not testify to "precisely the same type of [Pentecostal] religious experience."[128] In his annual report for 1913 and 1914, he rehearsed the fundamentally distinctive characteristics of the Alliance, among which was its existence as a "spiritual movement" that commissioned "only missionaries that [had] been baptized with the Holy Ghost."[129] Writing in the church season of Pentecost, Simpson encouraged his paper parish to contemplate "The Christ of Pentecost" who both was baptized with the Holy Spirit during his earthly days and continued to baptize all believers with the Holy Spirit during the present dispensation. As a concluding exhortation, he called his readers to "honor the Holy Ghost" as they "love[d] the Master."[130]

[127] See the "Official Statement of the Board of the Christian and Missionary Alliance Setting Forth Its Position with Reference to 'Tongues,' April 13, 1914." A copy of the document is in the AG Archives, Springfield, Mo. It consists of the text of a letter from A. B. Simpson to Dr. R. H. Glover, foreign secretary of the Alliance, dated April 13, 1914, included in the executive committee minutes of the Alliance Board of Managers for April 18, 1914 (no pagination). Simpson was advising Glover on how to deal with W. W. Simpson.

[128] His plea for toleration was made in the context of announcing with regret W. W. Simpson's departure from the Alliance over the issue of how far the "extreme views" of Pentecostals should be "pressed upon the people" ("Editorial," AW 42 [May 30, 1914]: 130).

[129] See the presidential report for 1913–14 as it appears in the "Annual Survey of the Christian and Missionary Alliance," AW 42 (May 30, 1914): 138.

[130] Simpson, "The Christ of Pentecost," AW 42 (June 13, 1914): 178–79, 182, esp. 182.

A "SEEKING" FOUNDER AND
A "SEEK NOT" DENOMINATION

The Tension Between Personal Renewal and
Organizational Consolidation

A review of the various stages of spiritual development in A. B. Simpson's life indicates that his inner posture was consistently one of a fervent seeker, desirous of experiencing ongoing spiritual renewal. The "Fourfold Gospel" was to him both the expression of the four cardinal biblical truths upon which he based his life and ministry and the historical description of his spiritual journey, which had been molded by contact with a succession of transdenominational movements prior to and following his departure from the Presbyterian Church in 1881. He was well aware of the turbulence invariably precipitated in his own person, his family, and among his friends by the interaction between the "present truths" that he came to embrace at critical turning points in his life and the past religious and theological traditions to which he had previously held. In the relentless pursuit of what he deemed spiritual truth his ecclesiastical identity underwent major redefinition. The resultant dislocation and loneliness from living a self-sensed prophetic life were once the subject of an address delivered in London, England. To a sympathetic audience he recounted the relational upheavals that were part and parcel of his spiritual pilgrimage:

Well do I remember when first the Holy Ghost came into my heart, how lonely I felt, how far I was removed from my old Christian associates—they could not understand me; but when I found one or two who did understand me, how dear they became to me! They were more than brothers, more than sisters. We could get closer because we could get deeper and higher in God's way. Then I remember how when I got a little further and found that this blessed Jesus is a living Christ, that not only is His spirit for my spirit, but His body for my body, touching mine into life, and holding and quickening it with His own resurrection life—then again I felt so lonesome. My old friends seemed to leave me, and for months I seemed to be alone, separated from hundreds and thousands of ministers and people I had loved and worked with all my life. But when one and two and three began to come and join this little band, oh how much deeper was the bond of love![1]

It was never Simpson's intention to establish another religious denomination. To the contrary, early Alliance constitutions, reinforced by his annual presidential addresses, repeatedly stressed the "catholic," nonsectarian, and ecumenical goals of the Alliance throughout the church at large.[2] Despite the demand for increased centralized administration brought on by growth, Simpson strove to perpetuate the vision of the Alliance as a nondenominational fraternity of like-minded spiritual pilgrims who verbalized their religious experiences and aspirations in terms of the Fourfold Gospel.

There were internal indications, however, that in the early 1900s some of the bedrock features of Alliance spirituality enshrined in the founder's own journey and writings were already on the wane. In 1906, Milton Bales, an Alliance field superintendent, assessed the trend toward holding "short conventions of from one to three days" as "a mistake." He called for them to be replaced with "fewer (if necessary), but longer conventions" that would provide sufficient time "to get souls through to God" and create

---

[1] As quoted in Thompson, *Simpson*, 63–64.

[2] See the original constitutions of the Christian Alliance and the Evangelical Missionary Alliance (1887) in WWW 9 (August and September 1887): 110, 111, and the International Missionary Alliance (1892) in Simpson, *Missionary Movement*, 35, as well as the "fraternal letter" included in the first annual report of the Christian and Missionary Alliance (1897) in AR (1897–98): 72, and the revised Alliance Constitution of 1912 in AR (1911–12): 39–40. Cf. Simpson's presidential addresses for 1911 and 1913 in AR (1911–12): 32–33; and AW 42 (May 30, 1914): 138.

the sustained meditative atmosphere in which spiritual conviction could "deepen."[3] More tellingly, in 1912 W. C. Stevens, principal of the Missionary Training Institute, declined an invitation to join the Alliance Board of Managers on the grounds of what he called "the ecclesiastical aspects of [the] work." He perceived the Alliance by this time as no longer a purely fraternal movement, but rather an organization caught in the process of departing from its traditionally "non-sectarian and interdenominational stance," which Simpson and his associates purportedly now found "impracticable." For Stevens, the fraternal principle was the only justification for the name "Alliance."[4] In 1914 Stevens was noted as "severing all official relations from the Alliance organization."[5]

Though Simpson's official public responses to Pentecostalism tended to be cautious, discerning of its errors, and wary of the potential of the new movement to seriously fracture the Alliance, thereby subverting the society's primary missionary agenda, his unofficial private writings and conversations told a somewhat different story. They held out the possibility of Pentecostalism being the means of a fresh visitation of the Spirit for himself and his followers. Many of his Alliance workers sensed the same opportunity to revitalize the Alliance through a new Pentecostal awakening. Thus they were prepared to receive and promote a Pentecostal baptism with tongues with the same depth of conviction as Simpson had previously done with the more controversial aspects of his Fourfold Gospel—sanctification and healing.

The Pentecostal doctrine of tongues as the initial evidence of Spirit baptism had at least as much biblical support as Simpson's radical understanding of healing in the atonement. Unlike his associates who joined the Pentecostal movement, however, Simpson was by this time no longer free to be simply a spiritual pilgrim who could embrace more "restored" truth, then separate, and join another renewal movement as he had done formerly. He now felt keenly the weight of shepherding and protecting the unity of an "Alliance" undergoing the process of de-

---

[3] See the "Report of Rev. Milton M. Bales, D.D., Field Superintendent," AR (1906): 37.

[4] See Stevens's letter of refusal dated February 2, 1912, in the executive committee minutes of the Alliance Board of Managers for February 2, 1912, 523–25.

[5] See the executive committee minutes of the Alliance Board of Managers for May 23, 1914, 1.

nominationalization (despite his denials). The demands of maintaining an expanding cadre of workers abroad who looked to him for guidance, as well as safeguarding considerable material and financial resources at home, were all-consuming. In this season of Simpson's life, the single-minded seeking disposition that had typified his earlier days could not ultimately displace the cautious conservative mind-set he came to develop as an ecclesiastical leader. Ironically, the excesses of Pentecostals in the early 1900s that preoccupied him in his public statements were in effect no worse than the controversial ragged fringes of the holiness and healing movement that had not deterred him from publicly identifying with it during the 1880s.[6] Furthermore, not all early Pentecostals agreed that tongues were necessarily the initial evidence of Spirit baptism.[7]

Immediately following Simpson's death in 1919, voices within the Alliance continued to call for spiritual renewal within the organization, a concern to which Simpson had not been oblivious as the Alliance entered its third decade. In 1921, E. J. Richards, secretary of the Home Department, observed a noticeable trend among "so-called full gospel workers to present the truth in such a way that it [did] not lead to definite conscious experience." Consequently many persons who subscribed to the Fourfold Gospel intellectually nonetheless failed to experience the power of the Holy Spirit in their lives with "satisfying fullness." The "clear and definite" inner witness of the Holy Spirit to one's regeneration and sanctification, which Richards regarded as essential to curb the inevitable drift into "worldliness and formalism," was conspicuously absent among a growing number of Alliance constituents.[8] In a similar vein, Paul Rader, Simpson's

---

[6] As a case in point see the relationship between Simpson and Frank Sandford, who built Shiloh, Maine. Sandford's deviance and demise is chronicled in Shirley Nelson, *Fair Clear and Terrible. The Story of Shiloh, Maine* (Latham, N.Y.: British American Publishing, 1989), esp. 46–48, 58; cf. the critique of "Elijah Sandford" by Simpson's colleague F. E. Marsh, "The Signs of the Times," in Philip Mauro et al., *The Signs of the Times*, 67–68.

[7] For example, see Minnie Abrams, "A Message from Mukti," *Confidence* (September 15, 1908): 14. For a full discussion of divergent views held by early Pentecostals, see Gary B. McGee, "Early Pentecostal Hermeneutics: Tongues as Evidence in the Book of Acts," and "Popular Expositions of Initial Evidence," in *Initial Evidence: Historical and Biblical Perspectives*, ed. G. B. McGee (Peabody: Hendrickson, 1991), 96–118.

[8] See E. J. Richards, "Report of Secretary of Home Department," AR (1920–21): 74, 75.

successor, highlighted the Alliance's departure from its spiritual roots and the resultant need to recover the "neglected truths" that had been the source of the movement's original success and vitality.[9]

For him, the new pressures and opportunities of the twentieth century could be countered and met effectively only by a return to "the old Apostolic Way" of spirituality, simplicity, and sacrifice.[10] Like Simpson in his closing years, Rader continued to insist, against the growing evidence to the contrary, that the Alliance, unlike denominational churches, was not held together by "ecclesiastical machinery," but was still an ecumenical "spiritual fellowship," deriving its bondedness from a united "common testimony of our glorious Lord." Somewhat nostalgically he claimed that the Alliance in the 1920s was still more "organism" than "organization."[11] As Alliance historians have noted, however, by this time the organization's drift away from its distinctive first-generation spirituality and character in the direction of mainstream evangelicalism was well underway, a trend that only accelerated as the twentieth century progressed.[12] Simpson's close friend and associate Kenneth Mackenzie, who outlived him by several decades, also acknowledged that Simpson's healing ministry had "slowed down" in later years. The trend continued until by 1937 "the note of healing," though "sounded loud and strong," met "no glad response" from Alliance people.[13]

The Revisionism of Aiden W. Tozer

In modern Alliance consciousness the widespread understanding of Simpson's posture toward Pentecostalism has been shaped more by the revisionist interpretation of A. W. Tozer (1897–1963) than by an analysis of Simpson's own writings. Tozer emerged as the Alliance's most distinguished personality in the twentieth

[9] Paul Rader, "Report of the President of the Christian and Missionary Alliance (1919–20)," AR (1919–20): 4f.

[10] Rader, "Annual Report of the President," AR (1922–23): 16.

[11] Rader, "Annual Report of the President," AR (1921–22): 12.

[12] In this regard see Wilson, "The Christian and Missionary Alliance: Developments and Modifications of Its Original Objectives," 374f.; and Reynolds, *Footprints*, 453–55.

[13] Kenneth Mackenzie, "My Memories of Dr. Simpson," AW 7 (July 24, 1937): 56.

century, acquiring a reputation through his pulpiteering and numerous publications that extended far beyond the confines of his Alliance audience.[14] The dominance of Tozer combined with the relative inaccessibility of many of Simpson's writings on Pentecostalism has left the former an authoritative Alliance interpreter of Simpson's views on the subject.

Tozer's biography of Simpson

In his biography of Simpson, published in 1943, Tozer attempted to distance completely the Alliance founder from Pentecostalism. In a particularly revealing paragraph, he rejected all possibility that Simpson might have possessed any affinity whatever for Pentecostal spirituality. He wrote caustically:

> The simple fact is that Mr. Simpson was miles out ahead of these people [Pentecostals] in his spiritual experience. He did not need anything they had. He had found a blessed secret far above anything these perfervid seekers after wonders could ever think or conceive.[15]

Tozer's "simple fact," however, hardly seems consistent with the evidence. Though Simpson's Nyack diary, which shows him to have been a seeker of Spirit baptism with tongues between 1907 and 1912, was made available to Tozer at the time of his writing the biography, he chose neither to mention nor to make use of it.[16] The image of the "seeking" Simpson was apparently not consistent with the impression of the Alliance founder that Tozer wished to leave in the minds of his readers.

Tozer's interpretation of Henry Wilson's trip

Tozer's version of Dr. Henry Wilson's visit to Alliance, Ohio, in 1907 to investigate Pentecostalism on Simpson's behalf

---

[14]Tozer served on the Alliance Board of Managers from 1941 to 1963 and was the vice-president of the Alliance from 1946 to 1950. He was elected editor of the *Alliance Weekly* in 1950 and made the publication famous for his editorials.

[15]A. W. Tozer, *Wingspread* (Harrisburg: Christian Publications, 1948), 133.

[16]For a physical description of the diary and confirmation that it was sent to Tozer, see John Sawin, "Simpson: The Man and the Movement," unpublished manuscript, section 1, 22.

also warrants further scrutiny. According to him, Wilson was unimpressed by what he observed and returned to New York with an ambivalent evaluation: "I am not able to approve the movement though I am willing to concede that there is probably something of God in it somewhere."[17] For Tozer this became the "crystallized utterance" of the Alliance.[18] A recent, officially commissioned history of the Alliance perpetuates Tozer's interpretation of Wilson's assessment of Pentecostalism.[19]

Tozer's uncorroborated report, however, is contradicted by other firsthand accounts. Simpson himself summarized the fruit of his trusted associate's trip to Ohio as confirming that "a deep spirit of revival" free from "fanaticism and excess" had broken out there.[20] W. A. Cramer, an Ohio superintendent, concurred. He stated that the "[Alliance] state workers and field superintendent, Dr. Henry Wilson from New York, were all in perfect accord with the testimony given by those who received their Pentecost, and expressed themselves in thorough sympathy with the experiences as witnessed in our midst."[21] Significantly, the Alliance Board of Managers' minutes tersely recorded that "Dr. Wilson's report of the work in Ohio was received with gratitude to God for his manifest blessing."[22] A Pentecostal editorialist claimed that as a result of Wilson's exposure to Pentecostal experiences among Alliance workers in Ohio, he promised to "report to the [Alliance] brethren at headquarters in New York, that this work is of God, and no man should put his hand upon it."[23]

---

[17]Tozer, *Wingspread*, 133. It is doubtful that Wilson actually visited Alliance, Ohio, since there was no Alliance work there.

[18]Ibid.

[19]See Niklaus et al., *All for Jesus*, 112.

[20]Simpson, "Editorial," CMAW 27 (April 6, 1907): 157.

[21]W. A. Cramer, "Pentecost in Cleveland," CMAW 27 (April 27, 1907): 201.

[22]See the executive committee minutes of the Alliance Board of Managers for March 30, 1907, 341.

[23]G. E. D., "An Influential Endorsement," *New Acts* (April 1907): 4. The periodical was started by Levi R. Lupton, who along with C. A. McKinney and Ivey Campbell made Alliance, Ohio, a center of Pentecostal influence in the northeast through their promotion of the annual camp meeting there. On Lupton's meteoric career, see Gary B. McGee, "Levi Lupton: A Forgotten Pioneer of Early Pentecostalism," *Faces of Renewal*, 192–208, esp. 195, 199. Lupton also reprinted the Alliance superintendent's (W. A. Cramer) report, "Pentecost at Cleveland," in *New Acts* (June 1907): 4, after it first appeared in Simpson's magazine.

Tozer's attitude toward Pentecostalism

The explanation for the substantial discrepancy between Tozer's interpretation of Wilson's 1907 Ohio tour and that of other sources may well lie in the projection of his strong anti-Pentecostal sentiments onto the past. By the time Tozer authored his biography of Simpson in the 1940s, Pentecostals had become to him "overheated souls" whose "ruling passion" was "not to win men to Christ, but to lead believers into" what he scorned as "their baptism." He denounced the "crass manifestations" of Pentecostals as a far cry from "the cultured heart of Simpson."[24] Despite the Alliance tradition of healing and evangelistic campaigns carried on by the Bosworth brothers during the 1920s, in which both numerous conversions and dramatic healings occurred, Tozer, in reaction to Pentecostal faith healers, prohibited all "professional 'healers' " from conducting special meetings in his church.[25]

In another of his Alliance biographies, Tozer used the life of missionary statesman Robert Jaffray to promote his own concept of the "sanctified" Christian life.[26] His portrait of Jaffray gave priority to the themes of evangelization, world missions, personal discipline, prayer, faith, passion, courage, vision, and the centrality of Scripture, but Tozer passed over the more charismatic dimensions of his life (see above, ch. 5).[27] The spirituality of the Alliance missionary was in effect selectively edited and recast in Tozer's image.

In his voluminous investigation of Tozer's theology of sanctification, Robert J. Patterson followed his observation of Tozer's antipathy toward the "tongues movement" with the startling conclusion that the Alliance giant differed with the official denominational concept of sanctification by crisis and was virtu-

---

[24]Tozer, Wingspread, 132.
[25]See David J. Fant, Jr., A. W. Tozer: A Twentieth Century Prophet (Harrisburg: Christian Publications, 1964), 85.
[26]A. W. Tozer, Let My People Go.
[27]See Robert J. Patterson's analysis of Tozer's biography of Jaffray in "The Life and Thought of A. W. Tozer Concerning Sanctification. An Investigation into the Thoughts of Aiden Wilson Tozer on the Doctrine of Sanctification and the Insights He Received from Some of the Past Mystics of the Church" (M.Th. thesis, Regent College, Vancouver, British Columbia, 1989), 290–94.

ally silent on "this key idea handed down by Dr. Simpson."[28] Had Tozer and Simpson been contemporaries, the latter might well have critiqued the former as a progressivist. While Tozer did preserve and popularize certain aspects of early Alliance deeper life teaching, including its less accepted mystical elements, the notion of a Spirit baptism subsequent to regeneration (which Simpson shared with Pentecostals) was somewhat diluted in Tozer's thought. In truth, pre-Protestant medieval mystics were much dearer to Tozer than were Pentecostals, though Simpson possessed a kinship with both traditions, albeit for different reasons.[29]

The "Seek Not Forbid Not" Statement of 1963

In 1963 the Board of Managers of the Christian and Missionary Alliance issued an official response to the spread of the charismatic movement among established non-Pentecostal denominations.[30] The content of the document consisted of a review of the Pentecostal controversy as it affected the Alliance in the early 1900s, a reproduction of the conclusion of Simpson's annual report for 1907–08 entitled "Special Revival Movements," and an assertion of the Alliance position on the gift of tongues. Preoccupied throughout with the extremism and divisiveness of early Pentecostals and more recent charismatics, the statement concluded with an appeal to Alliance clergy and laity to reject the initial evidence doctrine and to maintain an attitude toward tongues speaking of "seek not, forbid not."[31]

The statement "seek not, forbid not," not to be found anywhere in Simpson's writings, was most likely coined by A. W. Tozer, who was assigned the responsibility of preparing the final text.[32] In an attempt to convince its adherents of the historical

---

[28]Ibid., 432.

[29]See the preponderance of mystical treatises in Tozer's recommended reading list of spiritual classics in Fant, *Tozer*, 181; cf. his evaluation of the "finest devotional works" in *Keys to the Deeper Life* (Grand Rapids: Zondervan, 1957), 16–17.

[30]For the full text of the document see "Where We Stand on the Revived Tongues Movement," *Alliance Witness* 98 (May 1, 1963): 5–6, 19, and *Presence, Power, Praise: Documents on the Charismatic Renewal*, 3 vols., ed. Kilian McDonnell (Collegeville, Minn.: Liturgical Press, 1980), 1:63–69.

[31]"Where We Stand," *Alliance Witness* 98 (May 1, 1963), 19.

[32]See the Alliance Board of Managers' minutes for April 2–4, 1963,

continuity between its own views and those of Simpson, the denomination minimized if not ignored the tradition of its "seeking" founder, who though publicly critical of Pentecostal doctrinal and behavioral excesses nonetheless sought to create a climate of expectancy in which the full complement of first-century spiritual gifts could be restored to the modern church.[33] Subtle as it was, the departure of the 1963 Alliance statement from the totality of Simpson's original emphases is nevertheless apparent. In its official mid-century posture toward the charismatic movement, the denomination revealed, perhaps unwittingly, the extent to which it had changed from its founder as a result of its earlier encounter with Pentecostalism. Though over fifty years in the past, the painful crisis had not been forgotten, and the legacy left was a negative stereotype of the Pentecostal movement. This strengthened a cautious, defensive attitude toward any undue seeking of tongues and other spiritual gifts. The restorationist atmosphere endorsed and encouraged by Simpson and the early Alliance had disappeared.

2, 5. A pamphlet edition of the statement designed for public distribution concluded with an excerpt from Tozer's writings on the significance of Acts 2. See "Gift of Tongues. Seek Not Forbid Not—A Critique of the Revived Tongues Movement" (available from Alliance Headquarters in Colorado Springs, Colo.).

[33] For a stronger, unofficial Alliance statement which sought to distance the denomination even further from Pentecostalism and the charismatic movement, see Keith Bailey, "Dealing with the Charismatic" (Paper presented at the District Superintendents' Conference of the Christian and Missionary Alliance, February 28—March 2, 1977, Nyack, N.Y.; cf. my article, "Christian and Missionary Alliance (CMA)," DPCM, 164, 166.

SIMPSON'S NYACK DIARY*

May 1907 While preaching on Daniel, it came to me, like him, to set apart a time for prayer and fasting that God would specially bless the work entrusted to me and give me a special anointing of the Holy Ghost. I was the more led to do this in view of the approaching Council, May 29, and the special movement of the Holy Spirit abroad today, that God would show His will about it, and give to me all He has for me—and also for the work.

After one week of waiting on God I could not stop, but continued two, three, and up to the Council, and indeed with slight interruptions ever since.

I noted first a quiet but real quickening in my own soul, and great blessing in the Council. God kept us united, and at the close manifested Himself in some of the meetings in a very unusual way. There were several cases of the Gift of Tongues and other extraordinary manifestations, some of which were certainly genuine, while others appeared to partake somewhat of the

---

*A. B. Simpson, *Nyack Diary* (1907–16); unpublished typed copy of the original, is available in the archives of Canadian Bible College/Canadian Theological Seminary, Regina, Saskatchewan.

individual peculiarities and eccentricities of the subjects; so that I saw not only the working of the Spirit, but also a very distinct human element, not always edifying or profitable. And God led me to discern and hold quietly to the divine order for the gifts of the Spirit in I Cor. 12–14. At the same time I could not question the reality of the gifts, and I was led to pray much about it, and for God's highest will and glory in connection with it.

June

While attending the Ind.[?] Convention, on Saturday night, June 15, I was much in prayer and was reminded of God's meeting with me in this place in a remarkable way in 1881 and before and giving me a special message in 2 K. 13/18, 19. I again claimed it, and with it *all* His best will for me. I smote with *all* the arrows and asked in faith that nothing less than His perfect and mighty fullness might come into my life, and so testified on Sabbath morning, June 16 in the meeting.

I had come to this Conv. with much concern for the unity of our work. It was the first of the summer conventions and in a sense a sort of earnest of the others. The work here had been much split over the Tongues, and I had prayed much about it. God answered graciously and gave much blessing.

July 28

On the closing Saturday of the Nyack Convention I received, as I waited in the aftermeeting a distinct touch of the mighty power of the Holy Spirit—a kind of breaking through, accompanied by a sense of awe and a lighting up of my senses. It was as if a wedge of light and power were being driven through my inmost being and I all broken open [*sic*]. I welcomed it and felt disappointed when the meeting was abruptly closed by the leader, for I was conscious of a peculiar power resting upon us all and continuing to fill me. I carried it home with me, and for several days the deep sense remained as a sort of "weight of love," in addition to the ordinary and quiet sense of God I have felt so long.

August 9

On this Friday afternoon I retired, as I have done for so many years, to the place in the woods where God healed me in August 1881 and renewed my covenant of healing again as I have done every year since.

At the same time I pressed upon Him a new claim for a Mighty Baptism of the Holy Ghost in His complete Pentecostal fullness embracing all the gifts and graces of the Spirit for my special need at this time and for the new conditions and needs of my life and work. He met me as I lay upon my face before Him with a distinct illumination, and then as the Presence began to fade and I cried out to Him to stay, He bade me *believe* and take it all by simple faith as I had taken my healing 26 years before. I did so, and was enabled definitely to believe and claim it all and rest in Him.

Then He gave me distinctly Is. 49/8, "In an acceptable time have I heard thee, etc;" also Acts 1/5, "Ye shall be baptized with the Holy Ghost not many days hence." I knew that I had been baptized with the Holy Ghost before but I was made to understand that God had a deeper and fuller baptism for me and all that day and evening I was as sure of the Coming of His Spirit to me in great power as if I had already received the most wonderful manifestation of His presence.

I was accustomed at Old Orchard to spend hours every night waiting upon Him and praying about the meetings, and He often rested upon me in mighty realization and wondrously guided and blessed the work, but I felt there was MORE.

August 22 While waiting on God on my lawn at night as I have often done this summer, I had a special season of mighty prayer, in which God revealed to me the NAME of JESUS in special power and enabled me to plead it within the veil for an hour or more until it seemed to break down every barrier and to command all that I could ask. He also let me plead at great length Jer. 33:3 in the fullness of its meaning as God saw it, and to ask for "great and mighty things which I KNEW NOT." An utterly new revelation of His power and glory. He has let me know something of Himself, and for 26 years Christ has been in my bodily senses and members, but He has *much more.*

August 28 While waiting upon the Lord on my veranda, late at night, I ventured to ask Him for a special token of His giving me Matt. 6/17–18 and soon after He did give it in the form I asked, viz., a very mighty and continued resting of the Spirit down upon my body until it was almost overpowering and continued during much of the night. I accepted it and told Him I would take the promise in simple faith and not hesitate to believe that it was all for me. I had been timid at times about dictating to the Holy Spirit who is *sovereign* in the bestowal of His gifts, but now I fully take all that is promised in HIS NAME.

Aug. 23, 27, 30 Three remarkable seasons of prayer, fellowship, and blessing and Phil. 3/ given afterwards at night in a most marked way so that I was compelled to give up my previous message for the following Sabbath and take this for two following Sabbaths, Sept. 1, 8.

Again, Sept. 3, 4, 5, after much conflict, great deliverance and rest given and clear light.

One afternoon it seemed as if heaven was opened and I was permitted to see myself seated with Christ in the heavenlies within the veil and having the right to use His Name in victorious faith and prayer even as He. I can never forget this sense of *"the heavenlies"* and my place of right and power and acceptance there. Eph. I, II.

Sept. 5 Today the words *Zech.* 9:12 were distinctly given. The stronghold is the Name of Jesus and the power of the Holy Ghost. Lord show me what the *"Double"* means, all Thy estimate of it, the Double portion of the Spirit. Double all Thou hast ever done for me. Give me *Elisha's* blessing, the first born's portion—all Thy gifts and all Thy graces.

At night in my quiet sanctuary God came, and after a great conflict gave me a great deliverance and perfect rest and blessing.

Today and tomorrow set apart in fasting and prayer and wholly given up to God in waiting upon Him as far as other duties allowed.

Sept. 6   As I continued waiting on God today and spending the forenoon in the woods, God gave me clearly Acts 12/16, "Peter continued knocking." It has meant much to me. God would keep me still knocking. It is the third degree of prayer—the prayer that overcomes and opens. Along with it came clearly Ps. 132/ and Is. 62/1, with the same lesson, in evening prayer.

Later in the evening there came such a resting down of God's power for an hour or more at Prayer.

Sept. 8   Sabbath preached Ph. III and on way home such a revelation of Christ as I read last chapter of Luke and John and Rev. I, IV–VIII—The Lamb. To think that He, amid the glories of the Throne, should so come to me!!

Sept. 9   Left today for a few days quiet in Hamilton where I was ordained 42 years ago, September 12.

Sept. 12   Am giving these days to wait on God and asking Him to meet me and ordain me anew. He gave me today distinctly Nahum 1/15 for this season and I am claiming it. Also Jno. 15/16 and 17/22. I go to wait on Him for all.

On the way He woke me on the train at night for an hour of prayer and as I pleaded the Name of Jesus within the veil there was such a giving way of the barriers and such a coming in of God. Praise to His Holy Name!

Sept. 10   Arrived in Hamilton, spent the afternoon on my face in deep prayer in the Spirit. The Lord gave me Joel 2/26–8 for these days of waiting.

Sept. 12   Spent yesterday much in prayer and today wholly in fasting and prayer. Ordination anniversary—

The Lord provided an altar—Left a Memorial Stone of record. God's eye will be upon it always. "Cov—Witness Pent. HS? Anniversary. God"—

At 3–5 special service in memory—1865. Asked God to accept my offering and ordain me anew. The Spirit came with a baptism of Holy laughter for an hour or more and I am waiting for all He has yet to give and manifest.

Sept. 13   Awoke with deep burden of prayer, especially for K. The anniversary of [   ] much blessing in a season of prayer [   ] her at 10–11 and a baptism of divine love and power.

In the afternoon and evening a new burden came over me and as I prayed a general heal, a distinct sense of [   ] warmth—at times a penetrating fire—filled my whole body. I would have called it fever but God showed me most plainly that it was the Holy Ghost. It continued for about 6 hours even when I was not praying. I got alone with God much of the time and on my face opened all my being to Him to fill.

Left H. at 7 p.m. thanking Him that He had answered prayer and begun to ordain me in a new way and [   ] new power.

In the train I retired at 8 and continued in prayer till 10 or 11 with an increasing sense of God's nearness.

As I prayed in the Name of Jesus that He would let me lose nothing of His blessing, the Spirit came in me and moved sensibly and at last settled down within me with a mighty sense of rest, reality, and joy and Ps. 134.

Sept. 14   Returned with a great spiritual blessing. Woke after a night in which the Spirit had rested on me with glorious peace. The only word that expressed it was "The Lord in the midst of thee is mighty. He will rest in His love. He will rejoice over thee with singing."

At the same time there was a deep sense of much more to come and that my heart could not be satisfied without all the fullness of His power. The prayer went up spontaneously for all His fullness and power and the promise repeated itself over and over again, "Ask in my Name. Ask — rec. that your joy may be full."

At night an awful weight came over me and a deep conflict, but I think it was the enemy and as I kept abiding in Jesus there was peace.

Oct. 6
1912   Five years have passed since these mem. were written. Much has come and gone. God has been ever with me and wrought for me.

No extraordinary manifestation of the Spirit in tongues or similar gifts has come. Many of my friends have received such manifestations, but mine has still been a life of [   ] fellowship and service. At all times my spirit has been open to God for anything He might be pleased to reveal or bestow. But He has met me still with the old touch and spiritual sense, and in distinct and marked answers to believing prayer in my practical life.

Three years ago He permitted me to go to South America and brought me through great dangers. Two years ago He gave me great blessing in England. This year I spent my ordination Anniversary at Nyack in a very solemn season of waiting on Him and He met me. He bade me ask the Double Portion and showed me that I was to receive it as Elisha by faith and realize it in actual manifestation of God in my life and work. I fully believed for it and ever since have found Him [   ] in a new and gracious way. First in my preaching and teaching. Have had a new vision of truth and a new unction in preaching the last three weeks, also in teaching my classes at Nyack.

Next in deliverance and blessing. Prayer answered in a dangerous fall, also in regard to money. Have now several very hard places which only the God of Elisha can meet.

1. The new Inst. Bldg. Rec'd $20,000. All [   ] have failed. He must help—

2. The work at D [   ] St. W. are losing 500 a mo. and already 14,000 in arrears—I have been simply a silent and helpless partner and sufferer in it. He has loaned $3000 through prayer but some complete reconstruction is necessary. Am asking Him to give it.

3. My own business affairs heavily burdened by debt. Lord enable pay all He will.

3. Our missionary work needs increased funds much.

4. Possible visit to England after July.

5. Am under a heavy burden of prayer these days and nights.

[   ]   Have read with deep interest these memorials. This
14, 1916   year has been unparalleled in suffering and testing,
           and in answered prayer. At present I need God as never
           before. I am older and need new life etc. There are new
           forces and spirits in the work and things are harder.
           But God has done for me wondrous things this year in
           financial help, physical strength, and victory over the
           enemy in men and angels. I never so needed Him. I am
           taking him now in Jesus' Name for deliverance from a
           difficult financial burden so that I shall be set free from
           financial obligations that tie me up in my freedom and
           keep me in [   ]. Jesus will see me through. Also
           prayer for Council, summer conventions and my way
           plain. Also my head, heart, and life.

           God has wrought miracles of providence for me. Rest.
           D [   ] Sale lands Nyack. Rent of 260. New Rest. Leon-
           ard St. Inc. A. Pr. Co. Sale 692 8th Ave. Leg. [   ] and
           deliverance C B & Mrs. M— Praise. Also Howard.

           But O Lord help now in great need upon me.

           And [   ] give me fullness Spirit to [   ] and over-
           come and [   ] all situations around me.

aeg
11–21–42*

----

*This copy of Simpson's Nyack diary was typed from the origi-
nal by Miss Alda Greely, secretary to Alliance President H. M. Shuman,
on November 21, 1942.

EXCERPTS* FROM SIMPSON'S PRESIDENTIAL REPORT (1906–1907)

Revival

And this has been the blessed distinction of the year just closed. It has been a year of revival, a year of the Holy Ghost, "a year of the right hand of the Most High," bringing to every department of our Alliance work "times of refreshing from the presence of the Lord," and bringing nearer to our faith and hope the still better "times" of restitution of all things, of which God hath spoken by all His Holy prophets since the world began.

The baptism which came to our Institute in the early autumn was but a widening wave from the floods of blessing which were already watering our mission fields in India, China and Japan. And this in turn has still more widely spread over many other portions of our home field throughout the United States and Canada.

. . . . .

Special Manifestations

Some of the manifestations of the Spirit have been unusual and Pentecostal. Others have called for much caution and

---

*Excerpts from Simpson's "Annual Report of President and General Superintendent of the Christian and Missionary Alliance," AR (1906–07): 5–7.

spiritual discernment. In many places there has been apparently a revival of the gift of tongues, accompanied by genuine marks of the presence "of the Spirit of power, love and a sound mind." But these manifestations in other cases have been accompanied by extravagance, excess and serious error; have fallen into the hands of unwise and undesirable leaders, and have led to an undue magnifying of spiritual gifts and to many unscriptural teachings. In several instances the gift of tongues has been emphasized as an essential evidence of the baptism of the Holy Spirit, and believers have been led to seek for it rather than to seek the Lord Himself. Of course this has led to division, fanaticism, confusion and almost every evil work. But where wise leaders have guarded against extremes and aimed to preserve the "spirit of a sound mind" as well as the "spirit of power" there has no doubt been a deepening of spiritual life and a salutary impression upon the world for the things of God. As the shadow follows the light, so Satan loves "when the sons of God come to present themselves before the Lord," to come also. We must not allow the counterfeit to depreciate the genuine gold, neither must we be ignorant of the adversary's devices, or deceived by his wiles. Our attitude toward this movement has been at once the spirit of candor and the spirit of caution, and we believe that as we are enabled thus to stand we shall "keep the unity of the Spirit in the bond of peace," and have all that God has for us without the admixture of error and evil.

EXCERPT* FROM SIMPSON'S PRESIDENTIAL REPORT (1907–1908)

5. Special Revival Movements

A year ago reference was made in our Annual Report to the special outpouring of the Spirit in many places, accompanied by "speaking in tongues."

At that time attention was called to the great need of our maintaining the spirit at once of candor and caution—openness on the one hand to all that God had to give us, and watchfulness on the other hand against counterfeits, extravagances and false teachings. During the year this movement has developed on lines which more and more emphasize the need for both these attitudes. We believe there can be no doubt that in many cases remarkable outpourings of the Holy Spirit have been accompanied with genuine instances of the gift of tongues and many extraordinary manifestations. This has occurred both in our own land and in some of our foreign missions. Many of these experiences appear not only to be genuine but accompanied by a spirit of deep humility, earnestness and soberness and free from extravagance and error. And it is admitted that in many of the branches and states where this movement has been strongly developed and wisely directed, there has been a marked deepening of the spiri-

---

*Excerpt from Simpson's "Annual Report of President and General Superintendent of the Christian and Missionary Alliance," AR (1907–08): 9–13.

tual life of our members and an encouraging increase in their missionary zeal and liberality. It would, therefore, be a very serious matter for any candid Christian to pass a wholesale criticism or condemnation upon such movements or presume to "limit the Holy One of Israel."

But at the same time and with increasing intensity, there are other developments which make it very plain that those who have been made shepherds of the flocks of God and stewards of the mysteries of Christ, have need to guard with firm and fearless hand God's truth and work, seeking from Him the spirit of "discernment concerning things that differ" and carefully guarding the little flock from seducing spirits and false teachers.

One of these greatest errors is a disposition to make special manifestations an evidence of the baptism of the Holy Ghost, giving to them the name of Pentecost as though none had received the spirit of Pentecost but those who had the power to speak in tongues, thus leading many sincere Christians to cast away their confidence, and plunging them in perplexity and darkness, or causing them to seek after special manifestations of other than God Himself. Another grave tendency is the disposition to turn aside from the great trust which God has given to us in the salvation of sinners and the sanctification of believers, and seek rather for signs and wonders and special manifestations.

When we seek anything less than God we are sure to miss His highest blessing and likely to fall into side issues and serious errors.

Another evil is the spirit of separation and controversy and the turning away of many of our people from the work to which God called them, to follow some novel teaching or some new leader, perhaps little known or tried. In several cases our Alliance work has been almost broken up by these diversions and distractions, and many have forgotten their pledges for the work of evangelization and become involved in separation and often in bitterness and strife. Surely the Spirit of Pentecost is the spirit of peace and love and holy unity, and when we fully receive His baptism we shall be like them of old, of one accord and one soul.

Another result of the influence of which we have been speaking has been the sending forth of bodies of inexperienced and self-appointed missionaries to foreign lands under the honest impression on their part that God had given them the tongue of the people to whom they were to minister the Gospel. Without preparation, without proper leadership, and without any reasonable support, several of these parties have gone out to heathen lands only to find themselves stranded upon some foreign shore without the ability to speak any intelligible tongue, without the means of support, or even of returning home. These unhappy victims of some honest but misleading impression, have been thrown upon the charity of strangers, and after the greatest sufferings have in most cases with much difficulty, been compelled to return to their homes, disappointed, perplexed and heart-broken. In some cases our Alliance branches have been seriously disrupted by such outgoing parties, and a strain created which it will take years to heal. The temptation has come to new missionaries to abandon the study of the native language and wait vainly for some supernatural gift of tongues.

One of the most alarming tendencies of this movement has recently developed in several places in the form of a sort of prophetic authority which certain persons are claiming over the consciences of others and men and women are seeking counsel and guidance from them in the practical matters of private duty, instead of looking directly to the Anointing which they have received of Him and obeying God rather than men. It is said that in some instances Christian men and women go to these new prophets almost as the world goes to the clairvoyant and fortune-teller, and follow their advice with a slavish superstition that may easily run into all the dangers of the Romish confessional or the delusions of spiritualism.

These grave and distressing results have usually been averted in connection with our Alliance work where wise leaders have firmly held the work on Scriptural lines, giving perfect liberty for the working of the Holy Ghost in His sovereign will in the hearts and assemblies of His people, whether with or without these special manifestations, but at the same time holding the work and workers steadily to the directions of the Word, repressing all disorder, confusion, fanaticism and false teaching, keeping out unwise and untried leaders, and pursuing steadfastly the special work which God has committed to our hands, namely, the salvation of souls, the building up of believers and the evangelization of the world.

In this way, under the most critical conditions, our largest conventions and our strongest branches have been held in unity, order and spiritual power and blessing.

SIMPSON'S EDITORIALS

"Editorial," CMAW 27 (June 8, 1907): 205

Before the close of the Nyack Council it was evident there was a great hunger in the hearts of very many persons for a special manifestation of the presence and power of the Holy Spirit. The sober and well considered reports of many of our workers left no doubt that God is now visiting His people in many places, with a special manifestation of power quite unusual even in the most profound revivals of our time, and that while there has been much fanaticism there are undoubtedly well authenticated instances of the "gift of tongues" in connection with our work and meetings. Up to the present time there had been no manifestation of this kind in the Institute, although there had been very much prayer among the students respecting it. During the last night of the Council, however, an all night prayer meeting was held, and during this service the Holy Spirit came with great power upon all present. There were many prostrations and very many were led to seek God in deeper consecration and for greater blessing and power. One young lady received undoubtedly the "gift of tongues" and spoke in the language which some of the missionaries recognized as one of the dialects of the Congo. It was accompanied by every evidence of the mighty working of the Holy Spirit in the subject of this experience. The case was the more remarkable as she has been looking forward herself to mission work on the Congo. The meetings are still continued with profound and blessed results in the case of all who have been able to remain. We are glad to say that the attitude of the Council upon this important matter was one of great unity, the brethren fully accepting as genuine such manifestations as are characterized by the "spirit of power and of a sane mind," while at the same time standing together against the various forms of false teaching and wild excitement which are abroad on every side.

"Editorials," CMAW 28 (July 6, 1907): 313

The Toronto Convention has been a season of much bless-ing. The attendance was large, the Spirit earnest and united, the teaching in the power of the Holy Ghost and the missionary results most encouraging. Forty-two young people offered them-selves as candidates for the foreign field, and about $20,000 were pledged for missions, an offering much in advance of former records. The work in Toronto has passed through the new move-ment in connection with the gift of tongues without serious strain. There have been a few testimonies of God's special bless-ing in this direction, which have been frankly accepted as genu-ine, modest and entirely Scriptural, but the balance of truth has been carefully guarded. The work has been preserved from extrav-agance and excess and the "spirit of power and love and a sound mind" has been graciously poured out upon the work and the workers, and all hearts kept united in the great business of win-ning souls, exalting Christ and laboring for the evangelization of the world.

. . . . .

Some hasty and zealous people think that because they have received the gift of tongues or some special enduement of the Spirit, they must go out and join or form some new organiza-tion. This is a mistake. The Alliance movement stands for all the Scriptural manifestations of the Holy Ghost since Pentecost. Its peculiar testimony has ever been for the supernatural. Because we seek to guard against wildfire and fanaticism, and against handing over our meetings to leaders of doubtful character and scenes of disorder and confusion, is no evidence of antagonism to any and all the operations of the Spirit of Pentecost. That Spirit Himself has bidden us "try the Spirits whether they be of God," and has given us as the tests of His true working: decency, order, self-control, soberness, edification, and above all else, love. Give us these and then welcome to all the dynamite of God. No, beloved, stay with your brethren; avoid divisions and help one another to rise to all the height and power and blessing God has for us.

. . . . .

The more the Lord honors us with His gifts, let us be the more humble, gentle and sweet. Let us remember that "the greatest of these is love," and that censoriousness, self-consciousness, self-importance, and a spirit of criticism and division will counteract all the value of any gift of power or ministry. The supreme test of the Holy Spirit's operations is Christlike holiness and love.

"Editorial," AW 37 (January 27, 1912): 258

From time to time we hear expressions which lead us to believe that there is still a good deal of misapprehension in the minds of well meaning friends about the attitude of this paper and the Alliance movement toward what is generally known as the Pentecostal movement. We have heard it stated recently there has been of late a decided change in the attitude of the work and that it is unfriendly, if not hostile. This is a gross misrepresentation and must, at least in some cases, be intentional. Again and again it has been stated in these columns that we recognize the gift of tongues as one of the apostolic manifestations of the Holy Spirit which may be expected throughout the Christian age, and that we believe that at the present time it has pleased God to manifest Himself in this way to very many of His children in a thoroughly Scriptural and sane way and that the experience connected with it has really deepened their spiritual life and increased their usefulness. This is true of many of our missionaries upon the foreign field and many of our workers at home. What we do protest against is the narrowness and uncharitableness of making this experience a standard for every other Christian and insisting that without this special gift of the Spirit no one has a right to claim the baptism of the Holy Ghost. This is most unscriptural and harmful. Of the nine special gifts distinctly recognized in the New Testament Scriptures, this is but one, and the very principle on which these enduements are bestowed is, "All these worketh that one Spirit Himself, distributing to each one severally as He will." We recognize the sovereignty of the Holy Ghost in bestowing upon His servants the gifts most needful for their particular ministry and then insisting upon that love which is the greatest of all and which will lead each one instead of judging his brethren to recognize the Holy Spirit in others in all the varieties of Christian experience.

"Editorial," AW 40 (September 6, 1913): 353–54

We learn with deep sorrow that there is a quiet but continuous movement in a number of places, originating, we believe in extreme leaders of what is known as the Pentecostal Movement, to turn away godly and useful members of the Christian and Missionary Alliance from their loyalty to the work and the faithful support of foreign mission workers for whom in many cases they have become responsible. As we have repeatedly said in these columns the Christian and Missionary Alliance is not opposed in any way whatever to the manifestation in a Scriptural and sane way of the gift of tongues. We recognize it as one of the gifts of the Spirit mentioned in the New Testament. The only position to which the Alliance is opposed is the extreme, uncharitable, and unscriptural view which would make this gift the only scriptural evidence of the baptism of the Holy Spirit. In view of the apostle's clear statements in I Corinthians xii:10: "To another divers kinds of tongues," and again, I Corinthians xii:30, "Do all speak with tongues?" it seems inconceivable that sober, scriptural Christians can be drawn into any such extreme position and led to take such an unbrotherly and uncharitable attitude toward great multitudes of the children of God who have not received this special manifestation of the sovereign working of the Spirit, but are manifestly anointed with the Holy Ghost and bringing forth all the fruits of the Spirit in life and service. In a number of instances our Alliance branches have been disturbed and seriously broken by these extreme teachings and agitations, and we believe an effort is being made to establish some kind of religious movement of which the fundamental principle will be the exclusive doctrine above referred to. We can only guard our friends against these spiritual dangers with great faithfulness and yet with the utmost tenderness. Many of our beloved Alliance workers both at home and on the foreign field have received from the Lord this special manifestation of speaking in tongues, and their fellowship with God and their usefulness in prayer and service have been deepened and strengthened by the experience, but those of them that have been most richly blessed have been most emphatic and pronounced in their protest against the extreme position to which we have referred above. It would surely be very unlike the Spirit of God to weaken the interest of any Christian in the salvation of souls and the evangelization of the world. Surely the more filled we are with the Holy Ghost, the more will we be free from spiritual selfishness and loyal to the great trust of saving men, sending forth the Gospel, and bringing back the King.

INDEX OF NAMES